# INTERROBANG PREACHING

*(re)Discovering the Communication Secrets of Jesus*

DR. DOUGLAS WITHERUP

ISBN: 0692277579
ISBN 13: 9780692277577
Library of Congress Control Number: 2014915675
Interrobang Press, Kannapolis, NC

# WHAT OTHERS ARE SAYING

*In recent years we have seen the tribes of worship leaders and missional leaders in the church be awakened and empowered, with great results. Interrobang Preaching calls out to the tribe of preachers to rise up and embrace their calling with both renewed passion and renewed style to reach this generation.*

-**Mark Batterson**, New York Times bestselling author of *The Circle Maker* and Lead Pastor of National Community Church.

*We have come to expect every sermon to taper into a point, or two points, or three points. In Interrobang Preaching, Doug Witherup explores what might happen if sermons widened into conversations, or participations, or actions? This is a sparkling presentation on what it means to preach like Jesus.*

-**Leonard Sweet**, bestselling author, professor (George Fox University, Drew University), and chief contributor to sermons.com

*Training the current and next generation of preachers to communicate God's word with clarity and creativity is of utmost importance. In Interrobang Preaching, Doug will inspire and instruct you on how to do both.*

-**Rev. Wilfredo "Choco" De Jesús**, Senior Pastor of New Life Covenant Church and Author of *In the Gap and Amazing Faith.*

*Witherup's book will re-energize your message (and audience). It's a fun read that will transform your preaching as you use stories, images, and metaphors—just like Jesus.*

-**Nancy Duarte**, Author/CEO, Duarte, Inc.

*There are thousands of books on preaching—this one stands out! Doug will inspire you to preach with meaningful connection and lasting influence, while giving you a dramatic view of the greatest preacher of all.*

-**Dr. Kent Ingle**, President of Southeastern University and author of *This Adventure Called Life*

*Many sermons are high on information, but fall short on delivering an encounter with God. Doug effectively writes how to change this by showing how to preach with a SIM Card (story, image, and metaphor) and a surfboard (encounter). My challenge in the remaining years of ministry is to have my surfboard in one hand and my SIM card in the other.*

-**Rich Wilkerson**, Lead Pastor, Trinity Church, Miami and founder of Peacemakers International.

*I absolutely love what Doug Witherup has done with his book, Interrobang Preaching. His assessment and advice on effective communication hit the bull's-eye. True to his text, he uses the power of stories and imagery to bring concrete truths to life and application. That's the goal of every preacher. If you want to grow in your ability to share the greatest story of all time, invest in yourself by reading this book. Next time you speak you'll be glad you did. And so will your hearers.*

-**Scotty Gibbons**, communicator, coach, National Youth Ministries Strategist for the Assemblies of God, and author of *Overflow.*

*Communicating the Good News is not optional. Since the time of the Apostles to the end of time itself this amazing message must be shared. The challenge is just how to share this Gospel. ... Doug Witherup casts interesting angles on the challenge of communicating the Gospel in a contemporary society. His readable style, scholarly yet practical approach and relevance make this a book that I heartily* recommend to pastors, students and committed Christ-followers alike.

-**Paul R. Alexander**, PhD, President, Trinity Bible College and Graduate School, and author of *A Certain Life*

I've always been fascinated with hearing God, not in the audible realm but my inner life. Doug brings an important to message to those that "preach the Word". Doug gets right to the heart and makes a compelling case for experiencing God during preaching, both as preacher and learner. This book will inspire your passion to move people closer to God with the spoken Word.

-**Dr. Mike Rakes**, Lead Pastor of Winston-Salem First and church consultant for The Hardy Group

Doug Witherup uses creative ideas without compromising substance. He focuses on style while placing a high value upon what he calls the anointing of resonance. Interrobang Preaching takes us back to Jesus to move us forward in communicating a transforming message. It will be on my list of recommended reading for preachers.

-**Dr. Bob Rhoden**, Author of *Four Faces of a Leader*

*Doug is a creative and captivating communicator who will show you from Jesus' model how to do the same.*

-**Dr. Rick Ross**, Lead Pastor, Concord First Assembly

# *TABLE OF CONTENTS*

Acknowledgements · · · · · · · · · · · · · · · · · · · · · · · · · · · · · · xiii

Preface/ Introduction · · · · · · · · · · · · · · · · · · · · · · · · · xvii

Chapter 1   The Interrobang · · · · · · · · · · · · · · · · · · · · · 1

### 1st DIMENSION- DISPLAY
### What is the SIM Card?
### Tell the Story

Chapter 2   SIM Card Part 1: Story and Image · · · · · · · · · · · 17

Chapter 3   SIM Card Part 2: Metaphor · · · · · · · · · · · · · · · 30

Chapter 4   SIM Card Part 3: Country Music Preaching and
the Anointing of Resonance · · · · · · · · · · · · · · · 45

### 2nd DIMENSION - DISCOVERY
### What is the Interrobang?
### Guide into Mystery

Chapter 5   Interrobang Preaching
Part 1: Discovering the Mystery · · · · · · · · · · · · 57

Chapter 6   Interrobang Preaching Part 2:
Guiding Others into the Mystery · · · · · · · · · · · 70

## 3rd DIMENSION- DYNAMIC
### What is the Spirit Doing and How Can We Respond?
### Bring to Encounter

Chapter 7    Becoming a Spiritual Surfer · · · · · · · · · · · · · · · 87

Chapter 8    How to Preach as a Spiritual Surfer · · · · · · · · · 102

Chapter 9    Preaching in Spirals · · · · · · · · · · · · · · · · · · 123

Epilogue    The Story of a Wandering Preacher · · · · · · · · · · ·131

Notes · · · · · · · · · · · · · · · · · · · · · · · · · · · · · · · · · 137

*To mom.*

*Unless a kernel of wheat falls to the ground and dies,*
*it remains alone.*
*But its death will produce many new kernels—a plentiful harvest*
*of new lives.*
*(John 12:24).*

*I love you. Get the horses ready. I'll see you soon.*

# ACKNOWLEDGEMENTS

As far as words on a page, this book began as a part of my doctoral studies, but the heart of it began in 2000 with a seemingly coincidental encounter with a friend and fellow staff member in the front of our church auditorium. You can read the full story in the epilogue, but since that moment, I have been on a quest from the Lord to rediscover the power of preaching both in my life and in the ministry of the church as a whole.

In 2010, as I began my doctoral program at George Fox University under the lead mentorship of Leonard Sweet, the things the Lord had been speaking to me began to come to the surface with greater clarity and urgency. Beginning with our first time together as a cohort in Portland all the way to our final advance at Orcas Island, as Len spoke, he was singing the song that was in my heart. His ideas about preaching and so much of the assigned reading resonated deeply. So the words that follow are the result of a decade and half of what the Spirit of the Lord has been showing me in my life, sculpted and crafted in part through Len and my studies.

As I grow older, I value the relationships, friendships, and partnerships in my life more and more. Despite the labor that went into this project, relationships formed in the process outweigh its significance. People are greater than the product.

Thank you first of all to my wife Camden, who believed in me and supported me throughout. Her backing is like rocket-fuel in a writer's veins. My children, Cade and Ana, have kept my focus on what's important in life. Camden, you are a fruitful vine. Cade and Ana, you are olive shoots around our table.

Thanks to my mom and dad, who have provided for me a heritage far beyond the boyhood memories of playing baseball in the back yard. You have given me the gift of faith in Christ.

The team at GFES has been amazing. From day one my cohort was supported and poured into by faculty who were more than teachers. Len, thank you for teaching us to have "simplexic" faith on this journey. Cliff, thank you for encouragement, a gift on which no price tag can be placed. Loren, thank you for asking the hard questions.

I went into my studies expecting a degree. I've emerged with life-long friendships. My SFS10 tribe: Shane, Rick, Rob, Bryce, Matt, Danny, Len, Scott, Norb, Patrick, Paula, Scott, Gregg, and Tim, you guys have made this journey a blast.

Gwen Stowers, Joseph Phillips, and Frank and Kristin Cantadore, thank you for reading the manuscript and for your valuable input. Jon Hernandez, the cover design beautifully captures the spirit of interrobang.

As a junior in college, the Lord connected me with not only a great preacher, but someone who has become a mentor and friend. Joe Phillips, thanks for being all three.

Phil Bennett, the story in the epilogue is really the first chapter of the story. You continue to be a sage and spiritual guide in my life for which I am truly grateful.

cfa Preaching Team (Derrick, Jon, Anthony, Joe, David, and Stan)—for years the Conference room was our spot on Monday mornings. Who knew that we'd ever get around to writing sermons after all that football talk!

Doc Hackett, for decades you've been pouring into young preachers at Southeastern University. I was one of those you not only inspired with your teaching and preaching, but your life as well.

Every pastor needs a pastor. Rick Ross is that, and more. Pastor Rick, thank you for everything you've planted in me.

Dr. Kelly, you are a leader of leaders. Our tribe of the Assemblies of God in North Carolina is indebted to you as a spiritual father of our state.

# PREFACE/ INTRODUCTION

"Preaching should rank as the noblest work on earth."
-Andrew Blackwood[1]

For since in the wisdom of God the world through its
wisdom did not know him, it pleased God by the fool-
ishness of preaching to save them that believe.
1 Corinthians 1:21

The mantra in recent years has been, "everything rises and
falls on leadership." But what if leadership rises and falls on
communication? Specifically for pastors and those in ministry,
what if church leadership rises and falls on preaching?

There aren't many people who exemplify leadership more
than Andy Stanley. It takes exceptional leadership to plant
and grow a church to five campuses of over 24,000 people.
Andy is a gift to the church, and the Lord has used his books,
podcasts, and conferences to motivate and equip countless
spiritual leaders world-wide. But even church leadership-guru
Andy Stanley has said, "If we don't get Sunday morning right,
nothing else matters." Steven Furtick, pastor of one of the

fastest growing movements in the U.S., Elevation Church, made the statement to his congregation that his primary purpose is to communicate God's Word to them.

What both Stanley and Furtick understand is a key concept that's deeply rooted in the explosive growth of the early church described in Acts. The early church was multiplying at a rapid rate primarily due to the preaching and teaching ministry of the apostles. The Pharisees and religious leaders recognized the source of the catalytic young movement to be the preaching. Thus, they set about to shut it down by throwing the young preachers in jail, flogging them, and specifically warning them to stop preaching.

This experience simply added fuel to their fire and they continued to preach. What followed is a significant. The Greek Christians became upset that their widows were being overlooked in the daily distribution of food. This was a major internal conflict capable of causing the first church split. It required attention and leadership at the highest level. So the apostles became involved. Luke records what took place: "So the Twelve gathered all the disciples together and said, "It would not be right for us to neglect the ministry of the word of God in order to wait on tables. Brothers and sisters, choose seven men from among you who are known to be full of the Spirit and wisdom. We will turn this responsibility over to them and *[we] will give our attention to prayer and the ministry of the word*" (Acts 6:2-5, emphasis added).

Notice there are three things involved in this scenario: First, there is a leadership issue. Second, there is a social justice issue. Finally, there is the issue of prayer and preaching. Each of these dynamics is important and vies for the attention of the young church leaders. What they set forth is an intentional order of priority that is to serve as a template for the church to come:

1)  The vital importance of leadership
2)  The crucial importance of compassion ministry and social justice
3)  The *primary* importance of prayer and preaching

Furthermore, it is not coincidental that Luke connects the continued rapid multiplication of the church to the intentional primary focus on prayer and preaching. He records the church leaders' decision, then immediately gives the result: "So the word of God spread. The number of disciples in Jerusalem *increased rapidly*" (Acts 6:7, emphasis added).

---

*It's not coincidental that Luke connects the rapid multiplication of the church to the intentional primary focus on prayer and preaching.*

---

This may be a shocking statement, but leadership doesn't grow the church. The preaching of the gospel (birthed and bathed in prayer) is what grows the church. The early church grew through preaching and was sustained through leadership. Perhaps we've gotten the order reversed and have tried to grow the church through leadership and sustain it through preaching. It's not that leadership is unimportant. Without leadership, what is birthed cannot be sustained. Without leadership, the growth will fall apart. Leadership is vital because it raises up those with the spiritual gifts to create systems that undergird the church for continued health and growth. But leadership is not the driver. Skeptical? Think of the top growing churches. Yes, they are led by great leaders. But those leaders are primarily great communicators.

This isn't just theory or something that only worked 2000 years ago. As I've mentioned, both North Point (Andy Stanley) and Elevation (Steven Furtick) show what can happen when the leader finds his or her primary responsibility in communicating the gospel. I've also had the privilege of seeing this work first hand. The church where I serve on staff as a teaching pastor, Concord First Assembly, has grown from a single campus of 1300 to seven campuses of over 3700 in the past 10 years. Our Lead Pastor, Rick Ross, while possessing extraordinary leadership gifts, understands the primacy of preaching. Our model is founded on our preaching team and preaching calendar.

Every Monday at 9:00 a.m., the preaching team gathers together to work on the week's message. It is the first and most important thing we do all week. Furthermore, our church calendar flows out of our preaching calendar. Pastor Rick understands that if we don't get Sunday morning right, nothing else matters. And Sunday morning consists of worship and the word.

Think of it this way: a football team can have great leaders in place. They can do things behind the scenes such as branding, marketing, and television deals. They can structure meetings and even engage in strategic and meaningful community service. But if they don't win on Sunday, the rest of it doesn't work. On the other hand, if you've got a winning team that puts points on the scoreboard on Sunday, then everything else flows from there. The marketing guy's job is a whole lot easier. The community service is more meaningful. Sunday wins translate into weekday wins.

Do you remember hearing someone preach a powerful message and wondering, "Wouldn't it be great if God could use me like that?" Perhaps it was a sermon that so impacted your life, a sermon preached with such wisdom, passion, and anointing that you dreamed of being used by God in such a way. But years into ministry, buried under to-do lists and obligations, you've seen the joy of that dream and calling beginning to wane. What if we rediscovered the order of the early church? What if you began to place the most time, energy, and passion into prayer and preaching? And what if that subtle shift and return to the primacy of preaching began to fuel catalytic growth in the church once again?

The great preaching giant, D. Martyn Lloyd-Jones has said: "What is it that always heralds the dawn of a Reformation or Revival? It is renewed preaching. Not only a new interest in preaching, but a new kind of preaching."[2] That's what this book is about.

---

*"What is it that always heralds the dawn of a Reformation or Revival? It is renewed preaching. Not only a new interest in preaching, but a new kind of preaching."*
*-D. Martyn Lloyd-Jones*

---

Smith Wigglesworth prophesied there would be a wave of the Charismatic Movement, followed by a wave of a church-planting movement. Following this would be a wave of The Word and The Spirit. I believe this to be true. I believe it will be a movement of Spirit-empowered preaching that will usher in a Third Great Awakening. I believe that this Great Awakening will be global. And I believe it will be a work of God through not just one or two primary preachers named Edwards or Whitefield, but through the preaching of a tribe of preachers that the Lord is now raising up. We need both a renewed interest in preaching and a new kind of preaching. As you read, may the Spirit unlock and unleash a renewed calling and greater anointing in your life to communicate the greatest story ever told.

# CHAPTER ONE

## *THE INTERROBANG*

"With its preaching, Christianity stands or falls."
-P.T. Forsythe[1]

Whoever speaks must do so as one speaking the very words
of God.
1 Peter 4:11, NRSV

Jesus not only gave us the most beautiful, inspiring, and transformational message of all time, but he also gave us the best method to communicate that message. It will be our purpose to uncover and rediscover Jesus' interrobang communication secrets and for those truths to unlock and unleash transformation in you, your message, and your audience.

*I'm not a preacher. Can this book help me too?* Although the application of this book is directed to preachers, the truth is, we're all communicators of the gospel. Furthermore, the principles of Jesus' communication style apply across multiple disciplines—they work in the boardroom, the classroom, the sales room, and in every area of life. If you're a Sunday School teacher or small group leader, a businessman or salesperson, an administrator, educator, or in any other role requiring communication, Jesus' methods can help you. Simply put, if you want to become a better communicator, this book is for you.

So, exactly what is an interrobang and how does it apply to Jesus' preaching? I'm so glad you asked. Let's begin our journey of enthusiastic discovery.

## The Interrobang

Recently I attended a conference in Chicago dubbed as "fuel for the creative class." While I consider myself somewhat creative, I don't know that I have ever been described as "artsy," and there is a difference! Leading up to the event, based on the unusual Fairy-Tale-esque design of the promotional materials, I thought, "This is either going to be really good or really weird." As I entered the multi-level church building in downtown Chicago greeted by a young man dressed in seventeenth-century German garb, complete with suspenders and feather in his hat, playing the accordion, I leaned towards the latter. Thankfully, it turned out to be both.

The first keynote speaker was a man by the name of Bob Goff. Bob is a high-profile lawyer in Washington and an adjunct professor at Pepperdine, yet has given much of his life to pursuing justice for children in Uganda through an agency he founded known as Restore International. Bob is a fun-loving guy you can't help liking almost immediately. He has an "office" at Disneyland (sometimes he tells high-level executives to meet him at Tom Sawyer's Island), every Thursday he quits something, and he put his cell phone number in the back of his New York Times bestselling book, *Love Does,* and actually answers the calls!

Bob said many great things that morning, but one thing in particular leapt off of the stage and captivated my imagination. It is something I have not stopped thinking about since. In fact, as soon as he began talking about it, I started Googling it on my iPad and sketching a picture of it in my journal. I had the thought that if I didn't get anything else out of the entire conference, this one piece of information was worth it. (Not that I didn't enjoy the juice served later in the week by the masked, butterfly-winged person riding an eighteenth-century bicycle. *Did I mention the "weird" part?*) What did Bob mention that was so intriguing? The interrobang.

Here's the story. The year was 1962 and it had already been quite a year for the United States. John Glenn became the first American to reach outer space. The Kennedy administration successfully negotiated the Cuban missile crisis. And NASA launched AT&T's Telestar, the world's first telecommunications satellite, which has forever changed life on planet earth.

Against this backdrop of discovery, New York advertising executive and entrepreneur Martin K. Speckter found himself frustrated with his limited ability to communicate simultaneous excitement and curiosity. He felt handicapped by the lack of punctuation options. For Speckter, typing a question mark followed by an exclamation point (?!) was clunky and ugly.

Speckter set about to offer a solution. In an article he penned for a type-set magazine, he unveiled the first new punctuation mark in the English language in centuries: the interrobang. An "interrobang" is a hybrid question mark/ exclamation point.[2]

By themselves, the question mark and exclamation point are commonplace and ordinary, but when combined, wonder-twin powers activate! In tandem, they become one of the greatest symbols for twenty-first-century communicators. An interrobang is a symbol for enthusiastic discovery.

Interrobang is the thrilling combination of embarking upon a journey involving the unknown.

- Interrobang is the rush of adrenaline felt through clenched teeth and closed-eyes as your feet leave the dock, catapulting towards the cool water below.

- Interrobang is going to bed on Christmas Eve with the hopes the big red box behind the Christmas tree is exactly what you've been asking for.

- Interrobang is waking up to eight inches of snow and hearing your mom say the words, "No school today."

- Interrobang is the first paragraph of a mystery novel that commands your attention and beckons you to keep turning pages.

- Interrobang is the back door closing on the family car as you get ready to go on vacation to Disney World for the first time.

- Interrobang is the brush of hands on a date with the person you have found yourself falling for.

- Interrobang is walking over the sandy dunes and looking at the crashing waves of the ocean for the first time.

You don't know everything. But you have been given a taste. That taste ignites your senses and fills you with both excitement and wonder. Enthusiastic discovery.

Isn't that exactly what Jesus did? Think of Jesus' ministry. Crowds followed him to hear his message, at times pressing in so close he had to step into a boat for breathing room. People came to him expectant of a miracle, hoping to receive something life-changing. Through his life, his stories, his questions, and his miracles, he led person after person into the most enthusiastic discovery of their lives.

In fact, Jesus himself is the ultimate interrobang, the ultimate enthusiastic discovery. When you meet him, you are simultaneously "filled with joy *and* wonder."[3] Jesus is in chorus clarity and mystery. He is the answer and the question. He is the discovery and the road to discovery. Jesus both fills you with breath and takes your breath away, all at the same time. As you encounter Jesus, he leads you on the greatest page-turning adventure of your life.

And remember, Jesus not only provided us with the greatest message of all time, he also provided us with the greatest method to communicate that message. So let's go straight to the gospels to see what he did. In fact, that is exactly how this book began. Armed with nothing more than a parallel Bible of the gospels, a legal pad, and laptop, I set about to examine every preaching encounter of Jesus with the question: How did Jesus communicate in a way that so powerfully impacted the lives of his hearers?

Are you ready for the results? Here they are. Out of the 146 preaching encounters in the four gospels, Jesus used:[4]

| Method | Number of Times | Percentage |
|---|---|---|
| Teaching*<br><br>*It is interesting to note that Jesus only utilized direct teaching by itself ten times (7%). All of the other times were in combination with another methodology | 69 | 47% |
| Story/ Image/ Metaphor | 86 | 59% |
| Questions | 55 | 38% |
| Encounter Moments | 118 | 81% |

Throughout his life and ministry, in order to communicate the greatest message of all time, Jesus used story, mystery, and encounter. That's what interrobang preaching is.

Interrobang preaching is a rediscovery of story.

Interrobang preaching is a rediscovery of mystery.

Interrobang preaching is a rediscovery of encounter.

As the father of a six-year-old son and a four-year-old daughter, I feel like I'm a pretty good expert in the world of interrobang. My son, Cade, and daughter, Ana, live in the world of enthusiastic discovery. They have their hands on crayons, in paint, in dirt, or in Play-Doh. They are always asking "Why?" They're forever dressing up as princesses and Ninja Turtles. When I drop my kids off at school, I walk into a room full of interrobang kids. They're looking, touching, feeling, and asking questions. Each day is a blank canvas upon which they can learn something new and create something fantastic. They live in an interrobang world.

And you're an expert in the world of interrobang too. You were born to dream and play and discover. The problem occurs when we encounter tough situations and tough people that can sometimes cloud over our interrobang. But it's still in you.

Interrobang preaching is not about telling you what you're doing wrong. It's not even as much about telling you new things to do right. It's about unlocking and unleashing what is already in you. You were born to both live and tell a story. You were born to uncover and discover mystery. And you were born to encounter life and encounter Jesus.

Let's rediscover together. Let's take this opportunity to rediscover our inner interrobang and learn from Jesus how to lead others into their interrobang—the most enthusiastic discovery of their lives.

## What if?

I remember taking a family vacation to the Grand Canyon. We were already in Phoenix and loaded into the rental car to drive four hours north. I admit, as a dad, I had unrealistic expectations. Even though our kids were only four and two at the time, I was picturing the perfect family trip. We would probably sing songs together for the first part of the drive, stop halfway for a sunlit picnic in the path of a light breeze, and then climb back into the car whereby we would laugh the rest of the way there.

The problem was that my two-year-old didn't get the memo. She screamed quite a bit, which resulted in my driving full-speed down the interstate while simultaneously attempting to reach into the back seat to administer some fatherly discipline. I wasn't very successful and certainly shocked our babysitter, as was evidenced by her wide-eyed look in the rear-view mirror. Although she had known the Witherup family for years, I still don't think she had ever quite seen "Pastor Doug" lose it.

Even though the ride was a disaster, when we got to the Grand Canyon, one view made up for it all. I walked out toward the edge (not too close, mind you, as I'm not a fan of heights) and peered into the vastness of blue sky and rippled red ridges, trying to take in the enormity of the scene and experience. And I will never forget the inner voice of the Holy Spirit nudging me and whispering, "Doug, don't ever dream a small dream for me again." It was as if the Lord said, "Doug, if I can create this, nothing is too difficult for me."

It was an interrobang moment. Our inner interrobang should cause us to dream big dreams. Our inner interrobang should cause us to ask, "What if?" If the first layer of the interrobang is "enthusiastic discovery," then the second layer is "What if?" The beauty of Jesus is that he takes our "What ifs" of regret and turns them into "What ifs" of possibility.

Recently I had the honor of attending a dinner honoring the fiftieth year of Pastor Tommy Barnett's ministry. If there was ever an interrobang dreamer, it is Pastor Tommy. Not only does Tommy Barnett lead a congregation of over 10,000 in Phoenix, but he has also launched a ministry called The Dream Center in Los Angeles, which rescues drug addicts and prostitutes off the streets, gives them a place to stay, feeds them, provides job-training, and most importantly, introduces them to Jesus. Since its inception, Dream Centers have expanded and are now in New York, St. Louis, Australia, and all over the world. God has used Pastor Tommy to touch hundreds of thousands of lives.

As Pastor Tommy was speaking that evening, he mentioned how people will sometimes ask him, "Pastor Tommy, if you had it to do all over again, what would you do differently?" His response was stunning: "I would take bigger risks and dream bigger dreams."

---

*"If I had to do it all over again,*
*I would take bigger risks and dream bigger dreams."*
*-Pastor Tommy Barnett*

---

So why not dream a dream right now? Why not dream an interrobang dream? What if we began to ask "What if?"

- What if the Spirit renewed your heart, passion, and calling to preach the gospel once again?

- What if we rediscovered what it means to preach like Jesus?

- What if the Spirit breathed on our preaching once again and we began to see results like Jesus?

- What if the Spirit awakened the wide-eyed-with-wonder kindergarteners in our audience again?

- What if people began to come to church expecting an encounter with God?

- What if God gave us a renewed focus, renewed passion, renewed anointing, and renewed methodology that would inspire non-believers to know Christ and ignite believers to serve Christ?

In the following pages, we will go on an interrobang journey together. We will take out a lump of Play-Doh and enter a world of enthusiastic discovery. We will explore the preaching methodology of the greatest communicator who ever lived and recapture how to preach like Jesus.

Following Jesus' model, here are the three dimensions of Interrobang Preaching:

1st DIMENSION
What is the SIM Card?
(Tell the Story)

2<sup>nd</sup> DIMENSION
What is the Interrobang?
(Guide into Mystery)

3<sup>rd</sup> DIMENSION
What is the Spirit doing and how can we respond?
(Bring to Encounter)

As you rediscover how to preach like Jesus, may the fire and passion of your calling be re-ignited and fanned into flame. May you be raised up to preach with passion and anointing. May you see in your days a Third Great Awakening sweep our land.

# 1st DIMENSION- DISPLAY
## What is the SIM Card?
## Tell the Story

# CHAPTER TWO

# *SIM CARD PART 1: STORY AND IMAGE*

"The pulpit leads the world."
-Father Mapple in Moby Dick[1]

Trustworthy messengers refresh like snow in summer.
(Proverbs 13:25)

In their book, *Made to Stick,* Chip and Dan Heath tell the story of Elizabeth Newton, who earned her PhD in psychology at Stanford by studying people tapping out the melody to "Happy Birthday." (It kind of makes you think we should all sign up for Stanford PhD's!) In her experiment, Newton divided a group of people into two different groups: "tappers" and "listeners." The tappers were given a list of twenty-five well-known songs such as "Happy Birthday" or "The Star-Spangled Banner." The tappers were then asked to tap out the song and have the listener guess which song was being played as they knocked on the table. How many songs do you think the listeners were able to guess? The answer may surprise you.

Out of 120 tapped songs, the listeners guessed only three. That's it. Only 2.5 percent were guessed correctly. And these were not off-the-wall songs. This was Twinkle Twinkle Little Star!

As hard as those numbers are to believe, here is what made the experiment dissertation-worthy. Before they tapped out the song, the tappers were asked to predict whether or not the listener would be able to guess the song. Any idea what the tappers predicted? Here's a hint: it was higher—much higher. They predicted their listeners would guess correctly fifty percent of the time. That's quite a discrepancy. The tappers communicated effectively one time out of forty, but guessed that they were communicating effectively one time out of two![2]

I'm afraid that what Dr. Newton may have discovered is also a portrait of what is occurring in churches all over the world on Sunday mornings. As preachers, we have the song (our sermon) in our heads. We've received revelation from heaven and have been humming it all week long. We hum it in the shower and while drinking our morning coffee. We hum it on the way to work and in between meetings. The song is so familiar to us. The tune seems so obvious. Yet when we go to preach on Sunday mornings, we are limited to tapping. The audience doesn't have access to what is in our heads (thank goodness!) nor have they been pondering, brainstorming, and analyzing it all week long. Thus, at times, blank stares. From the pulpit, we are dumbfounded. "This is Twinkle, Twinkle Little Star, people! This is so obvious. How are you not getting this!" Tap, tap, tap, tap, tap, tap, tap. (At this point, it may be good to have someone else tap out a song for you.)

If you've ever experienced this frustration, imagine Jesus' frustration. Jesus not only had received revelation; Jesus was revelation. Jesus possessed infinite wisdom and was trying to communicate the fullness of God's love to finite humanity. It's no wonder phrases like, "Are you so dull?" sometimes came out of Jesus' mouth!

## How did Jesus Tap Out His Messages?

How did Jesus take on this challenge? How did the infinite God communicate with finite humanity? How did he, in three-and-a-half years, deliver a message of love, hope, and redemption that would forever change the course of humanity? That seems like a pretty big challenge.

The first dimension of interrobang preaching is that Jesus used a SIM card: he told **S**tories, showed **I**mages, and (re)signed **M**etaphors. Most of us realize Jesus told a lot of stories. What we may not fully grasp is the combination of story, image, and metaphor and how, when used together, becomes a powerful communication tool.[3]

---

*The parables were more than just stories;*
*they were SIM cards: Story, Image, and Metaphor.*

---

Jesus certainly understood the power of the SIM card. In fact, eighty-six of the 146 preaching encounters in the gospels record Jesus as telling a story, showing an image, or (re)signing a metaphor. That's almost sixty percent. Let's take a look at a couple of preaching encounters where Jesus utilized SIM cards.

All of the Synoptic Gospels record the parable of the soils. Mark's version reads:

He taught them many things by parables, and in his teaching said: "Listen! A farmer went out to sow his seed. As he was scattering the seed, some fell along the path, and the birds came and ate it up. Some fell on rocky places, where it did not have much soil. It sprang up quickly, because the soil was shallow. But when the sun came up, the plants were scorched, and they withered because they had no root. Other seed fell among thorns, which grew up and choked the plants, so that they did not bear grain. Still other seed fell on good soil. It came up, grew and produced a crop, some multiplying thirty, some sixty, some a hundred times" (Mark 4:2-8, NIV).

All three SIM-card elements can be noted in this parable. First, it is a story. The narrative is about a farmer who went out to sow seed. Second, there is imagery. The main images he uses here are seeds, soil, and the hindrances that keep the seed from growing (rocks, the scorching sun, and thorns). Finally, the story and the images combine to form a metaphor, where the seed represents the gospel, the soil represents the heart of humanity, and the obstacles represent the hindrances that keep the word from taking root and producing a good crop.

Another example can be seen in the parable of the lost coin. Luke records:

> Or suppose a woman has ten silver coins and loses one. Doesn't she light a lamp, sweep the house and search carefully until she finds it? And when she finds it, she calls her friends and neighbors together and says, "Rejoice with me; I have found my lost coin." In the same way, I tell you, there is rejoicing in the presence of the angels of God over one sinner who repents (Luke 15:8-10, NIV).

Again, we see all three SIM-card elements. There is the story of the woman losing and finding her coin. The image is of the coin, and the woman looking desperately for it. The coin metaphorically represents humanity's "lostness" and the woman represents the heart of the Father who is desperately searching for his lost people.

Let's dive into this a bit deeper and investigate further. Why are story, image, and metaphor so powerful as communication tools? What did Jesus know about these elements that led him to communicate so often with SIM cards?

## Story

In 2013, I didn't want to watch the Super Bowl for a couple of reasons. First and foremost, my Pittsburgh Steelers were not playing. Second, the Baltimore Ravens were playing. Now, there are a couple of rules about being a full-blooded, Terrible-Towel-waving Steeler-Nation fanatic: 1) root for the Steelers at all costs; and 2) root against the Ravens. Thus, when it became fairly obvious that the Steelers were not going to make a run at an NFL league-leading seventh Lombardi trophy, I intentionally scheduled a flight back from a conference during the Super Bowl. Yet, even my spiteful flight planning didn't keep me from catching some of the game. As I stood in the Atlanta airport viewing the game on one of the elevated airport screens, I noticed something. And it wasn't about the game. It was about the commercials.

Many people watch the Super Bowl for the game. Many others watch for the commercials. Throughout the years, field-goal-kicking horses and dancing babies have entertained the masses. But this year I noticed something deeper.

In 2013, a thirty-second commercial during the Big Game cost approximately four million dollars, which puts a ninety-second ad at twelve million. These companies assemble the best and brightest creative advertising minds they can find. They have ninety seconds to get out the message about why you should eat their nacho chips, drink their soda, or buy their car.

So what did they do? Let's take Jeep for example. Perhaps you remember the ad. I dare you to pull it up on YouTube and watch it without tears. There are images of servicemen and women in uniform. One father in his camouflage fatigues is shown looking down at his dog tags, which include a picture of his family back home. Wives are shown wiping tears from their eyes around the breakfast table. We see kids kneeling by their bedside praying for daddy or mommy to return home safely. Oprah narrates the scene. "There will be a seat left open. A light left on. A favorite dinner waiting. …There will be walks to take, swings to push, baths to give. …Because in your home, in our hearts, you've been missed. You've been needed. You've been cried for. Prayed for. …Because when you're home, we're more than a family, we're a nation that is whole again."

What did the Jeep advertising team do that was so effective? With the world watching, with one shot to inspire and convince men and women sitting in living rooms across America eating hot wings to buy a Jeep, what did they do? They told a story.

But it's just as important to realize what Jeep did not do. They didn't bombard us with bullet points and statistics. They didn't show photos of leather interiors and talk about heated seats. They didn't show us the engine with impressive stats about torque and horsepower and fuel economy. They didn't talk about the independent suspension and push-button four wheel drive. They told a story. While they told that story, we saw images of hopeful wives and eager children on their way to the airport riding in a Jeep to pick up daddy. Why? Jeep understands a truth many preachers do not: in order to motivate for a decision, we must first touch the emotions.

## Story & Science

In her book, *Wired for Story,* Lisa Cron talks about recent research in neuroscience that shows how our brains are actually hardwired to respond to story.[4] Cron explains that when we nodded off in seventh-grade history class as the teacher recited the entire list of German monarchs, but leaned in while hearing our grandfather tell a story from his childhood, "it's not because we are lazy…but because our neural circuitry is designed to crave story."[5] Furthermore, not only are our brains hardwired for story, but research also shows that our brains are re-wired by story. Powerful stories have a way of changing the way we think.[6] These are significant findings. While Jesus may not have had access to Cron's research, he certainly understood the human brain and how we learn best.[7]

If Cron's findings are true, then story cannot be relegated to illustrating points; story can *become* the point. Story is not merely something to be added to a sermon in support of the real truth, it becomes the real truth. According to Cron's research, not only can we learn through story, but we learn *best* through story. As author Annette Simmons tells us, in our day the mantra may well be, "Whoever tells the best stories wins."[8]

---

*"Whoever tells the best stories wins."*
*-Annette Simmons*

---

## How Did We Lose Story?

Intrinsically, we understand what Cron's research shows. Think about bedtime as a kid. Your dad didn't tell you to hop up in his lap so he could present "seven life lessons for today." He told you a story. Yet somewhere along the way, we grew up.

As we "matured" we somehow took on the belief that stories, while they make for nice introductions, cute illustrations, and memorable closers, are just add-ons. We felt the pressure to preach more adult-type sermons chock full of information and bullet points. Stories might work in kids church, but we are in big church now. Where did this line of thinking come from? Because it certainly didn't come from Jesus.

Centuries ago, the Greeks set forth a communication methodology of truth by proposition. Against the backdrop of a world that had been explained through myth, the emerging scientific minds basically said, "Hey, wait a minute. Fire probably didn't appear because some god stole it from a mountain and gave it to humans." There was probably a more rational explanation for its appearance. Because stories were the vehicles for myths, as people became more educated and enlightened, myths were rejected and story got thrown under the bus as well. Instead of telling stories, communicators began to use linear methodology, with a main idea being argued through a series of propositions.

Plato described "myth" untrustworthy. Years later, as the Gutenberg generation was solidifying, philosopher Thomas Hobbes wrote: "In connection with the rise of modern science the rejection of metaphor, symbol, and myth became explicit."[9] As the modern, scientific era came to prominence, there was a simultaneous rejection of story, image, and metaphor.[10]

---

*As the modern, scientific era came to prominence, there was a simultaneous rejection of story, image, and metaphor.*

---

In propositional communication methodology, stories, while encouraged, were used to illustrate (the word means "shed light on"). The real truth, the real meat of the message, was found in the points. Although propositional communicators allowed for story, it was in a way that was subservient to the points.[11] But that's not what Jesus was doing. Jesus was not using parables to illustrate propositional truths. Jesus' stories weren't used to illustrate the sermon; the SIM card *was* the sermon.[12]

Can I encourage you at this point to tell stories. Tell stories with confidence. You aren't simply providing a mental break during the "real preaching." You're not merely shedding light on the real truth of your message. You're not being cute, nor or are you succumbing to our entertainment culture. You are following the preaching methodology of Jesus himself, communicating to the human mind in the way it was wired to receive truth by the Creator-God. While your people are smiling or laughing or leaning in or wiping away a tear during a story, the Holy Spirit is at work re-wiring their brains and transforming their hearts! That's the power of story!

---

*While you tell stories, the Holy Spirit is at work re-wiring people's brains and transforming their hearts.*

---

## Image

One of the greatest things preachers could do to improve as communicators would be to visit a children's church service and watch a kids' pastor at work. Children's pastors utilize one of the best methods of communication: object lessons. The kids' pastor holds an apple and tells the story of Johnny

Appleseed. Then he or she proceeds to talk about the power of sowing and reaping. Kids watch. They pay attention.

But again, somewhere along the way we grew up. As good students of modernity, we learned that stories and pictures were kids' stuff, and that real learning occurs through empirical study and scientific method. Propositions replaced stories and arguments replaced images.[13]

However, in case you haven't noticed, we live in an increasingly visual culture. As Dr. Lynell Burmark in *Visual Literacy* writes, "Welcome to the age of images." Burmark goes on to say that "the primary literacy of the 21st century will be visual: pictures, graphics, images." And she has plenty of research to back up her claims. For instance, "of all our sense receptors, the eyes are the most powerful information conduit to the brain. They send information to the cerebral cortex through two optic nerves, each consisting of 1,000,000 nerve fibers. By comparison, each auditory nerve consists of a mere 30,000 fibers. Nerve cells devoted to visual processing … account for about 30% of the brain's cortex, compared to 8% for touch and 3% for hearing." This neuroscience is linked with research showing that "visual aids have been found to improve learning by up to 400%." Burmark shows there is a progression in the way we process information: "first the image, then the thoughts."[14]

---

*"Welcome to the age of images."*
*-Dr. Lynell Burmark*

---

Did you hear that? First the image, then the thoughts. Not, first the propositional statement, then the illustration. Therefore, don't be afraid to use visual aids as you tell your stories.[15] You're not being cute, gimmicky, or childish. You are communicating in a way modeled by Jesus, and in the way which God designed our brains to learn. So go ahead, tell a story, show an image, preach object lessons for adults!

# CHAPTER THREE

## *SIM CARD PART 2: METAPHOR*

"In every age of Christianity since John the Baptist
drew crowds into the dessert, there has been no
great religious movement, no restoration of Scripture
truth and reanimation of genuine piety, without new
power in preaching, both as cause and effect."
-John Broadus[1]

Trustworthy messengers refresh like snow in summer.
(Proverbs 13:25)

### Metaphor

Ever ask someone for the recipe for their out-of-this-world pineapple upside-down cake at a dinner party, only to receive it from them, make it, and have it not taste the same? Later you discover they neglected to give you the final "secret ingredient." With story and image, you're almost there. You're coming close to having your amazing, someone-will-ask-you-for-it-at-a-party SIM card recipe, but you're still missing the secret ingredient. We can tell good stories and effectively use images, but the secret sauce of the SIM card is metaphor.

---

*We can tell good stories and effectively use images, but the secret sauce of the SIM card is metaphor.*

---

Stories entertain, images stick, but metaphor changes everything. Imagine this: If I make the statement, "Schools are factories," your mind conjures up all kinds of images, such as brutal boredom in seventh grade algebra class. But if I say, "Schools are well-tended gardens," your mind goes in a different direction. Perhaps you think of an English teacher who encouraged you to write and who brought Shakespeare alive, making it understandable and entertaining. Simply by changing the metaphor, your perception of school is altered.

Or if I made the statement: "argument is war," you remember struggling to convince your stubborn four-year-old daughter that wearing footsie jammies to bed in August isn't a good idea and that she needs to change into summer jammies. After all, her summer jammies have princesses on them and she likes princesses. (Okay, maybe this just happens in my house.) But if I alter the metaphor to say, "argument is a dance," the entire scene changes. Now the thoughts are of you sitting comfortably at your favorite local coffee shop with a beloved friend discussing the role of the missional church over a latte. You offer an idea. Your friend listens. Your friend tells a story. You listen. Back and forth, give and take. There is respect, mutual movement, and appreciation for opposing positions. Again, the power of metaphor. By changing the metaphor, we change our thinking. By changing the metaphor, we change the world.[2]

---

*By changing the metaphor, we change the world.*

---

## Conduit Metaphors (How Metaphor Works)

Before turning on the skill saw in shop class and thrusting a 2 x 4 under a sharp blade rotating at warp speed, it's probably a good idea to listen to your shop teacher explain the power of the machine. (Oh, and by the way, if your shop teacher is missing half an index finger, you may want to drop the class immediately.) Metaphor is a powerful machine. So before we turn it on and lose a thumb, let's examine how it works.

Two of the experts in the world of metaphor are George Lakoff and Mark Johnson. (Yes, there are actually "metaphor experts!" In fact, there is an entire field of study around it known as semiotics.) Lakoff and Johnson describe how effective communication utilizes "conduit metaphors." In a conduit metaphor, there are three key aspects:

1) ideas are objects
2) linguistic expressions are containers
3) communication is sending

Thus, according to Lakoff and Johnson, "The speaker puts ideas (objects) into words (containers) and send them (along a conduit) to a hearer who takes the idea/objects out of the word/containers."[3]

Here is how I interpret these guys, who are way smarter than I am: "Hey, Kool-Aid!" Remember the Kool-Aid commercials? Thirsty kids on a hot summer day calling out for a drink of Kool-Aid? Suddenly Kool-Aid man bursts through a brick wall, bringing joy and refreshment to all. Now just where the brick wall came from, why Kool-Aid man decides to run through it rather than go around, and how he manages not to spill the Kool-Aid while performing this extraordinary feat of strength is a subject for another discussion, but the important thing is this: the Kool-Aid pitcher personifies what Lakoff and Johnson are talking about.

The kids on a hot summer day are your audience (Jesus speaks of people thirsting for the gospel). The Kool-Aid is your message. (Yes, the more Biblically-correct image would be water and no, I'm not asking people to "drink the Kool-Aid!"). In order to dispense the Kool-Aid to the thirsty children, you could cup your hands and attempt to throw the liquid at them with minimal amount of success (and unhappy mothers), or you could use a container. The container allows you to deliver the contents with much greater efficiency, not to mention happier moms since you avoided spilling Kool-Aid on their children and provided them a refreshing beverage with less sugar than soda.

In fact, Kool-Aid man personifies the entire SIM card.

- The metaphor is the container. (You transmit ideas through conduit metaphors.)
- The image is that of the Kool-Aid man. (I bet at the end of this chapter, you'll remember the picture of this guy.)

- The story is the smile. (The story is what causes your audience to engage, to lean in.)

## SIM cards are Kool-Aid pitchers.[4]

One of the greatest thinkers/authors/communicators of the last century, C.S. Lewis, talked about the power of communicating with master metaphor. That's what a SIM card is. A SIM card is a Kool-Aid pitcher that serves as a container for your entire message. A SIM card is not an illustration for your message; a SIM card is your message.

## Active Volcano Metaphors

James Geary has written a brilliant book on the power of metaphor entitled *I is an Other: The Secret Life of Metaphor.* In it, Geary talks about the power of what he calls "active volcano metaphors." A volcano can be one of three things: active, dormant, or extinct. An active volcano is alive, bubbling with force and energy. A dormant volcano once had active power, but is now simply an external structure devoid of impact. An extinct volcano is just that: extinct. It is a "museum piece" that people may look at or study. It has no potential for eruption. Geary applies the volcano analogy to metaphors by offering three examples:

- Extinct metaphors: "I see what you mean."
- Dormant metaphors: "We're getting in over our heads."
- Active metaphors: "Laughter is the mind sneezing."

If you're like me, you didn't even realize the first was a metaphor. The second barely conjures an image. But the phrase, "laughter is the mind sneezing" immediately evokes a picture and stimulates thought. It is fresh and creative.

Which category do most of our preaching metaphors fall into? While they may not necessarily be extinct, perhaps many are dormant. How many times have we heard the death of Christ explained with a judiciary metaphor? I'm not arguing against the theology of these metaphors; I just think they're dormant. They evoke as much emotion as saying, "We're getting in over our heads," and create as much of a stir as a dormant volcano.

When you think "dormant volcano" metaphors, think church signs or Christian bumper stickers:

- When God closes a door, He opens a window.
- Body piercing saved my life.
- Be an organ donor. Give your heart to Jesus.
- Christ is our steering wheel, not our spare tire.

Cliché. Trite. Overused. But while dormant metaphors cause eye-rolls, active-volcano metaphors are eye-openers. They grab us, shake us, catch us off guard, and pique our curiosity. One of the crucial questions for our preaching as we move forward is, "What are the active metaphors?" What are the new metaphors we can use to stimulate the imagination, stir the emotion, and make people think? What is the next generation of active-volcano metaphors—metaphors that are bubbling with energy and power?

> *While dormant metaphors cause eye-rolls,*
> *active-volcano metaphors are eye-openers.*

## From Outlines to SIM Cards

Let's get practical here. I'm talking Monday-morning-coffee-shop-sermon-prep-mode practical. What does preaching with a SIM card look like from Monday-morning prep to Sunday-morning delivery?

It's quite simple, really. In the propositional methodology of modernity, we began with a text and asked the question, "What is the main idea?" Then we set forth to argue the truth of that idea through a series of points (propositions) with some stories (illustrations) thrown in for good measure. A good sermon began with a good outline, as follows:

Main Idea:

I.   Point One

    A. Explain the Biblical Text
    B. Illustrate the Biblical Text
    C. Apply the Biblical Text

II.  Point Two (You get the idea.)

With SIM card preaching, you also begin with the biblical story, but your first question as you read through the text is, "What is the SIM card? What is the Story/ Image/ Metaphor?"

For example, let's look at the passage in Luke 1 of Mary's visit to Elizabeth and draw the SIM card out of the text. The story reads:

> At that time Mary got ready and hurried to a town in the hill country of Judea, where she entered Zechariah's home and greeted Elizabeth. When Elizabeth heard Mary's greeting, the baby leaped in her womb, and Elizabeth was filled with the Holy Spirit. In a loud voice she exclaimed: "Blessed are you among women, and blessed is the child you will bear! But why am I so favored, that the mother of my Lord should come to me? As soon as the sound of your greeting reached my ears, the baby in my womb leaped for joy. Blessed is she who has believed that the Lord would fulfill his promises to her!" (Luke 1:39-45)

I preached this message to a group of leaders and the SIM card I used was this:

## Story

I told the story of the famous symphony conductor, Benjamin Zander. One of the keys to success for Zander lies in the fact that good conductors don't make a sound. A conductor's power lies in his/her ability to make other people powerful. Zander then makes the statement: "My job is to awaken possibility in other people."[5]

## Image

While I was telling the story, I had a conductor's baton that I carried with me on stage.

## Metaphor

The metaphor was this: as leaders, we are conductors. Our power is to awaken possibility in the lives of those around us.

See how the SIM card replaces the propositional statement and becomes the container for the message? The audience leans in to listen to the story of Benjamin Zander. They will remember the image of the baton. Their thinking is changed by the metaphor of a conductor. (Leadership is not expertly playing a trumpet and having people follow you; leadership is putting down the trumpet, picking up a baton, and drawing out the trumpet player in someone else.)

Notice also that we're not reading the SIM card back into the biblical story. We are simply harvesting the SIM card from the biblical story. There was something about Mary (the power of Christ within her) that, when she was around Elizabeth, caused what was within Elizabeth to awaken. Mary's "power" was awakening possibility in others. What enabled Mary to do this? Here are some of the points I used to add structure and support to the SIM card:

- Conductors are overflowing with the Holy Spirit (v. 41)

- Conductors strategically connect with others (v. 44)

- Conductors call forth the destiny in people (v. 42)

*Isn't this the same thing as propositional preaching? You are still using points.* The difference is subtle, but significant. First of all, you are using a SIM card instead of a main idea. Truth is not a proposition to be argued, but a story to be heard, an image to be seen, and a metaphor to be grasped. Second, stories don't illustrate the real meat of the sermon (the points); now points simply add some structure to the real meat of the sermon: the SIM card. Begin with the SIM card, weave the SIM card throughout the message, and close with the SIM card.

---

*Truth is not a proposition to be argued, but a story to be heard, an image to be seen, and a metaphor to be grasped.*

---

Here are some further examples of master SIM cards:

## The Kintsukuroi Tribe[6]

Kintsukuroi is an ancient Japanese art form whereby a broken piece of pottery is repaired with gold or silver lacquer, *with the understanding that the piece is more beautiful for having been broken.* (I encourage you to Google "kintsukuroi" to see an image.) That will preach! I used this SIM card in a message I preached called "The Kintsukuroi Tribe."

My main Biblical story was the man with the shriveled hand in the temple in Matthew 12. The Pharisees and Jesus enter the temple. While the Pharisees are looking to exploit this man's weakness for their benefit, Jesus tells the man to stretch forth his hand. When he does, the shriveled hand is healed. I proceeded to talk about the fact that:

1) We all have weaknesses.

The brokenness of the man's hand was obvious, but he wasn't the only one in the room with a weakness. Regardless of how visible or hidden they may be, we all have areas of hurt, weakness, and brokenness.

2) Our weakness doesn't detract from our value.

Jesus declared that this man is valuable. What is interesting about the statement is the timing. Jesus ascribed worth to the man *before* he was healed. We're not just valuable to God once we have it all together. Sometimes our beauty is in our brokenness. "But we have this treasure in jars of clay to show that this all-surpassing power is from God and not from us" (2 Corinthians 4:7). "But he said to me, 'My grace is sufficient for you, for my power is made perfect in weakness.' Therefore

I will boast all the more gladly about my weaknesses, so that Christ's power may rest on me" (I Corinthians 12:9).

3) What we reveal (instead of conceal) Jesus can heal.

I don't imagine the man with the shriveled hand was too excited when Jesus asked him to stretch forth his hand. Most of us don't like to reveal our weaknesses. In fact, since our days in middle school, we've become experts in trying to conceal our flaws. But what we conceal, we continue to live with. What we reveal to Jesus is exposed to his power and healing.

We are all a Kinsukuroi Tribe. We all have weaknesses. Our weakness doesn't detract from our value (there is beauty in our brokenness). And what we reveal, Jesus can heal. Again, see how the SIM card was not merely an illustration for the message, but became the message. Kintsukuroi was the master metaphor that formed the container for the entire sermon.

## Living Bridges

In northeast India, a giant cliff leads into a hidden world—a placed called Meghalaya. At one and a half miles high and hit by constant monsoons, Meghalaya (whose name means "the abode of clouds") is possibly the wettest place on the planet.

Once, a world-record 25 meters of rain fell in one year alone. Nearly all the rain falls during the summer months, causing gentle streams to become raging rivers and making them almost impossible to cross. However, crossing these rivers is key for survival of the tribe. So how do they do it? How do they cross during monsoon season?

They begin by planting a tree called a strangler fig. First, the trees' tangled roots prevent the bank of the river from washing away. Then, they coax the roots across the stream, a process that takes over 30 years. When they reach the other side, the roots take hold there, forming the basis of a structure that will survive any deluge: a living bridge.

We used this as a SIM card for an entire series through the book of John based on the theme passage, "By this everyone will know that you are my disciples, if you love one another" (John 13:35). We asked the question, what is the church known for? We then proceeded to preach a series of messages talking about how we are to be living bridges. Together, through unity, love, and the power of the Holy Spirit, we form living bridges that connect people to Christ.

The first dimension of interrobang preaching is to read the passage of scripture with the question: What is the SIM card? This SIM card then becomes the container for the message. Remember, you were born to both live and tell a story.

1st DIMENSION
What is the SIM Card?
(Tell the Story)

## CHAPTER FOUR

## *SIM CARD PART 3: COUNTRY MUSIC PREACHING AND THE ANOINTING OF RESONANCE*

So turn it on, turn it up, and sing along
This is real; this is your life in a song
Yeah this is country music
- Brad Paisley

A word fitly spoken is like apples of gold in a setting of silver.
Proverbs 25:11, ESV

### Country-Music Preaching

I was born in the north. As such, I didn't develop a taste for country music. In fact, quite the opposite; I couldn't stand it. When I travelled with a college group one summer, arguments arose over the music played in the van. I and my fellow northerners couldn't understand how the southerners liked country music. Eight years later, I married one—a southern girl that is. And as a good husband, when my southern-belle bride turned on country music in the car, I would listen. And then, it hit me. I couldn't believe it. These people were singing about my life! I heard songs about swimming at the neighborhood swimming hole, eating at Grandma's after church, learning to drive on back-country roads, and Bo Duke sliding across the hood of the General Lee. This was my childhood. I was hooked. If you sing a song about my life, I'm going to listen.

Country musicians are brilliant storytellers. Love it or hate it—that's why country music is so popular. Country musicians sing stories about people's lives. They operate in what I call an anointing of resonance. They put lyric and music to the tune that is already in our heads. So we listen. Then, we do something even greater—we sing along.

Even though I am a converted country-music fan, I still don't make a habit out of watching Taylor Swift concerts. But one day as I walked through my living room, Taylor was on TV performing an outdoor mini-concert. As I watched, something amazing happened. A crowd of teenage girls were singing along—and not just passively mind you, but passionately. They were singing so loudly you could hear them over the hundred-thousand-dollar sound system. What drove the passion in their sing-along? I suggest it was more than just seeing their idol on stage. It was because Taylor was singing the story of their lives. They weren't singing Taylor's story; they were singing their story. The anointing of resonance.[1]

What does all of this have to do with preaching? Quite a bit, actually. Most preachers would be more than happy to know their audience is listening. Considering the internal distractions of wandering minds and external distractions of wandering thumbs (on smartphones), just holding someone's attention for thirty minutes is a challenge. But great preachers go beyond just getting people to listen. Great preachers get people to sing along. They operate in the anointing of resonance.

## The Science of Resonance

If you walked into a room with a partially-opened baby grand and looked at the strings of the piano as someone on the other side of the room struck a perfect "C" on a tuning fork, you would see the C string on the piano vibrate without anyone striking the piano's key. Why is this? The answer is resonance.

Technically speaking, any object that is free to vibrate tends to do so at a specific rate, which is the object's resonant frequency. This phenomenon occurs when the object is submitted to a frequency equal to its natural frequency.[2] You may have witnessed this when driving down the road and hearing something on the dash rattle at a certain speed. That is because the particular speed you are driving at emits the same resonant frequencies inherent in a particular part of your dash. If you slow down or speed up just a few miles per hour, the rattling stops.

In 1940, a suspension bridge at Puget Sound Narrows in Tacoma, Washington collapsed during wind gusts. However, the wind did not blow the bridge down. Rather the wind caused the bridge to vibrate at its natural frequency. Because of this phenomenon, soldiers actually break step when they are crossing a bridge.[3]

Or have you ever wondered why you feel so relaxed at the ocean? Sure, being miles away from the office has something to do with it, but so does resonance. Ocean waves have the a frequency of approximately twelve cycles per minute, the same as your breathing during the deepest parts of your sleep. As you relax with your toes in the sand, listening to the crashing waves, your body is literally resonating with the ocean.

Search "resonance" on YouTube. One video shows salt crystals forming brilliant geometric patterns as they are subjected to different frequencies.[4] In fact, there is such a great connection between science and resonance that brilliant scientist Nikola Tesla has said, "If you want to find the secrets of the universe, think in terms of energy, frequency, and vibration."[5]

---

*"If you want to find the secrets of the universe, think in terms of energy, frequency, and vibration."*
*-Nikola Tesla*

---

## The Theology of Resonance

What would lead science to say so many "secrets" of the universe have to do with resonance? Let's go back to the beginning, to the creation of the world. When God created the heavens and the earth, the spoken word activated creation. Genesis 1 records nine "And God said" moments. God spoke, and it was so—light, water, land, vegetation, and so forth. According to the imagery of Genesis, everything we see began as vibrations in the vocal chords of God.

Let's put our interrobang glasses on and continue to follow this trail of discovery. John adds to the discussion as he begins his gospel in a parallel manner to Genesis, speaking about the creation of world. What John adds to the Genesis account is the revelation of Christ and his presence and work as part of creation. John's gospel begins, "In the beginning was the Word, and the Word was with God, and the Word was God" (John 1:1). John tells us that Christ was with God from the beginning.

Now, let's move one step further to Paul's record of the creation account. He writes in Colossians,

[Christ] existed before anything was created and he is supreme over all creation, for through him God created everything
in the heavenly realms and on earth.

He made the things we can see
and the things we can't see—
such as thrones, kingdoms, rulers, and authorities in the
unseen world.
Everything was created through him and for him.

He existed before anything else,
and he holds all creation together (Colossians 1:15-17).

The apostle gives us great insight here. When the Lord
spoke the world into existence, he did so in and through *the*
Word: Christ. The words of God were spoken through The
Word of God. Everything was created in Christ and through
Christ and for Christ. There is a very real sense in which Christ
is in all things and through all things. That is why the ultimate
resonance is the resonance of Christ.

---

*In Creation, the words of God were spoken in
and through The Word of God.
That is why the ultimate resonance is the resonance of Christ.*

---

Preaching in its highest sense is speaking a word
in alignment with what the Spirit is already speaking in
people's lives. When we do this, we sing the note that
strikes the chord in someone's heart. Our job is not to argue
someone to faith; our job is to speak a word of resonance.

As we do, the Spirit, who is already at work within them, brings that word to life.

## The Anointing of Resonance

The question then becomes: How? How do we speak words that resonate? The answer, in part, goes back to our country musician friends. Remember, they don't just get people to listen. They get people to sing along. Worship shouldn't be the only participatory sport on Sunday mornings; we can turn sermons into sing-alongs as well. Here are a couple of suggestions on how to be a country-music preacher:

1) Pay attention

Fascinating stories are all around you. I used to believe that preachers with captivating stories simply had extraordinary things happen to them. But this isn't necessarily true. Great storytellers pay attention. Great storytellers are first of all great noticers.

I was teaching a master's course on Biblical methods of preaching in Washington D.C. We were at Ebenezers, Mark Batterson's coffee shop a block away from Union Station. During the week, the class took several field trips throughout the city, such as to the National Museum of Art and the Capitol. Before we went out, I told the class that a week in D.C. should equip them with enough stories, images, and metaphors to fill their preaching bag for a year. Washington D.C. is SIM City. There are stories of courageous men and women who formed and shaped our country. There are statues, buildings, and works of art that serve as powerful images. They combine to form metaphors that transform the way people think and live. For instance, at the National Museum of Art, we saw a series of four paintings by Thomas Cole entitled "The Voyage of Life," which depicted the four stages of life: childhood, youth, adult, and old age. Batterson and National Community Church used this SIM card for an entire sermon series.

*Well, sure, if I lived in DC I'd find great SIM cards too!* But what we have to realize is that we all live in SIM City. Fascinating stories, rich images, and life-changing metaphors are in our backyards and right down the street. So while the answer to SIM City is that we live there; the problem is, we live there. In other words, if you live in Florida, you probably don't go to Disney World until you have friends visiting from out of town. It's only when guests come that you realize, "Oh yeah, we live right down the street from Mickey Mouse."

I have a good friend that talks about "living as a tourist in his hometown." What a great idea. There are places all around you that are full of SIM cards. Why not make a list of the top 10 things someone from out of town would want to do if they visited your state? Then take a week and go do them. Go on a "Preachers Field Trip." I bet you'll come back with a year's worth of SIM cards.

## 2) Write things down

Someone has said the shortest pencil is greater than the longest memory. *But I'll remember that story.* No you won't. When it comes time for the sermon into which the story fits perfectly, you will have forgotten. Even if you do happen to remember the gist of the story, you will have forgotten details that make the story vivid and bring it to life. Whether you are a paper-and-pen journaler or an Evernote user, find a way to write down your stories.

## 3) Harvest native stories

Which is better: a freshly-plucked strawberry purchased from a road-side stand in June, or one bought at the supermarket in January? Exactly. Ditto for stories. Books and Google can be sources of great stories, but they are imports. The best stories for your congregation are locally grown and harvested. Whereas the first suggestion had more to do with places and things, this has to do with people. Everyone has a story. Listen to people. Listen to their stories. (Hint: You can't listen if you're always talking!)

Regardless of what pre-set stations are programmed into your car stereo or which iTunes playlist is getting the most air time, when it comes to preaching, you need to be a country-music preacher. Tell stories that resonate. When you do, you will move beyond capturing people's attention to getting them to sing along.

In modernity we made a point. In this new era, we must tell stories, show images, and (re)-sign metaphors. Interrobang Preaching begins with harvesting the SIM card.

---

*In modernity, we made a point.*
*In this new era we must tell stories, show images, and (re)-sign*
*metaphors.*

---

2nd DIMENSION: DISCOVERY
What is the Interrobang?
Guide into Mystery

# CHAPTER FIVE

## *INTERROBANG PREACHING PART 1: DISCOVERING THE MYSTERY*

"Anyone can memorize facts and figures.
The only way to really learn is to get out
there and experience something.
Let your curiosity lead you."
-Ted from *Curious George*

A reliable messenger brings healing.
Proverbs 13:17

As with many things in my life, I was a latecomer to the first edition of the television show *24*—about a decade late, in fact. It all started when my wife and I had the idea of getting rid of cable and saving money by getting high-speed internet and Netflix. (Four months later we ended up with both and paying more money than ever, but that's another story.) Looking for a show to watch after putting the kids to bed, we landed on *24*. A couple of episodes was all it took. Like kids who tasted ice cream for the first time, we were hooked. What was the cause? Sure, the storyline was good. And yes, as with most American males, I now wanted to be Jack Bauer. But the addiction-causing, can't-stop-watching-until-one-a.m. power of *24* is in its interrobang brilliance. What *24* does better than perhaps any other show is weave together multiple mysteries. As soon as you unravel one, you uncover three more threads of the mystery. We couldn't stop watching.

The creators of *24* understand the power of mystery and the power of questions. In the first dimension of interrobang preaching, we uncovered the power of the SIM card. Now, we explore the dimension of questions and mystery.

## Jesus and Interrobangs

As you read through the gospels, perhaps you've noticed how often Jesus asked questions. It's quite a bit. In fact, out of Jesus' 146 preaching encounters, he asked questions in 55 of those encounters. That's almost forty percent. It's pretty amazing when you think about it. The one who created the universe, the wisest person who ever lived (sorry, Solomon), the one who had the answer to every question before it was even asked, asked questions of other people.

This seems counter-intuitive. Jesus knew the answer to everything. He knew the answer to every Biblical question, every theological question, and every life question anyone could ever have. If you had fifteen minutes with Jesus, wouldn't you be the one asking him questions? Wouldn't Jesus be the one wanting to give the answers? Jesus only had three and a half years of public ministry on this planet. That's not a lot of time. So you would think he would spend as much time as possible unloading and downloading anything and everything he knew. You would think he would have the disciples staying up late and getting up early while he lectured, followed by plenty of pop quizzes and essay tests. But he doesn't. Instead, the Omniscient One becomes the Questioner, the All-Knowing becomes the All-Asking. The question for us is, why? Why would Jesus ask so many questions? What did Jesus know about humanity, about discovery, and about communication that caused him to end so many of his sentences with question marks?

---

*What did Jesus understand about humanity, about discovery, and about communication that caused him to end so many of his sentences with question marks?*

---

Part of the answer is found in a particular passage in Luke. In this account, Jesus went from town to town preaching the gospel. He's accompanied by his disciples as well as an inner circle of financially-supporting women. As he and his team embarked on their evangelistic tour, Jesus told stories. He used the parable of a farmer going out to scatter seed, with some of the seed falling on different types of soil, each yielding a different result. At the conclusion of his message, the disciples approached Jesus and asked him to explain the meaning of the parable.

Before responding to their request, Jesus inserted this interesting statement: "He said, 'The knowledge of the secrets of the kingdom of God has been given to you'" (Luke 10:10).

Is Jesus saying the kingdom of God is a secret? Now I'm even more confused. "Wait a minute Jesus, I thought you came to earth to reveal yourself? I thought the idea was that people would come to see more clearly, not become more confused? I thought proclaiming the gospel was about getting the word out, not about keeping a secret? If we wanted to keep this a secret, I can think of a whole lot of easier methods than traveling long distances on foot while trying to avoid people who want to kill us!"

Conrad Gempf offers an explanation. In his book *Jesus Asked,* Gempf notes that the word translated "secret" by the NIV is probably not the best translation. The Greek word used here is *musterion.* Any guesses as to its English equivalent? Bingo. "Mystery."[1] And the difference is huge. With a secret, facts or knowledge are withheld. The goal is of a secret is, needless to say, to keep it a secret. But a mystery is different. With a mystery, the facts are there, but a person must engage in a purposeful quest to understand the mystery. The answer is not unattainable, but it requires effort. Gempf believes Jesus wants his hearers to engage in a quest for themselves, and to begin to uncover the mystery of God's kingdom.

Jesus is not keeping a secret. Jesus is engaged in interrobang preaching. Jesus is leading people on the most enthusiastic discovery of their lives. Jesus is placing a lump of Play-Doh in people's hands, calling out their inner kindergartener, and saying, "Let's engage in a story together that will lead you into step after step of wide-eyed wonder. This isn't a story you simply listen to; this is a story you are involved in. You're not just a reader, you're a character."

## Jesus and Questions

As we investigate the world of Jesus' questions, we find a couple of layers.

A story about Jesus and Philip reveals them in greater detail. The context of the story is the feeding of the 5000. The crowd had been listening to Jesus all day and is hungry. John's account reads, "When Jesus looked up and saw a great crowd coming toward him, he said to Philip, 'Where shall we buy bread for these people to eat?'"[2] At this point, we're rooting for Philip. The inner-VBS student who knows the outcome of the story cheers, "Come on Philip! You got this. Find the kid with the lunch. Make a bold statement of faith! This is your moment, Philip!" Philip answers, "Eight months' wages would not buy enough bread for each to have one bite!"[3] Cue Debbie-Downer music.

Philip fails. Or does he? Interestingly, this is the only behind-the-scenes glimpse where a gospel writer overtly states *why* Jesus asked a particular question. John continues, "He asked this only to test him, for he already had in his mind what he was going to do."[4] Did you catch that? The question was a test. Jesus already knew what he was going to do. He is not asking Philip for advice because he is stumped and needs input. Jesus is not circling the disciples around a white board for a brainstorming session. As someone has said, "When Jesus asks you a question, it's not because He doesn't know the answer!"

Not only does Jesus know the solution to the problem, but Jesus knows what is inside Philip. Jesus asks a question because he wants Philip to see what is inside Philip. If Philip realizes what's going on inside his head, this can be a moment of growth for the young disciple. Though Philip may have gotten a red "X" next to his answer on paper, all is not lost. If Philip utilizes this question to discover some of the mystery within himself, it is a win.

In scripture, we see other examples of this type of questioning as well.[5] For example:

- As part of the Sermon on the Mount, Jesus asks, "If you love those who love you what reward will you get? Are not even the tax collectors doing that?"[6]

- On a boat with his disciples, after they are soaked and shaking from a storm, Jesus asks, "You of little faith, why are you so afraid?"[7]

- After finishing a teaching on eating his flesh and drinking his blood which prompted a mass-exodus of his followers and grumbling by the Twelve, Jesus asks, "Does this offend you?"[8]

- On a ministry trip to the villages of Philippi, Jesus asks, "Who do people say the son of man is? Who do you say that I am?"[9]

With each of these questions, Jesus compels the listener to look inward. "What do I believe? What is the state of my soul? Why am I acting the way that I am?" In other words, "What's going on within the mystery of me?" Jesus asks some very blunt questions, uncomfortable questions, because Jesus understands the power of a question to cut to the heart and force the listener to confront reality within.

Not only does Jesus ask questions that lead people into some serious soul-searching and self-discovery, but Jesus asks other questions as well. Sometimes Jesus asks questions in connection with SIM cards:

- Connected to the parable of the Good Samaritan, Jesus asks, "Which of these three do you think was a neighbor to the man who fell into the hands of robbers?"[10]

- Connected to the story of the watchful servant, Jesus asks, "Who then is the faithful and wise manager, whom the master puts in charge of his servants to give them their food allowance at the proper time?"[11]

- Connected to the parable of the two sons, Jesus asks, "Which of the two did what his father wanted?"[12]

What is Jesus doing here? Is there purposeful connection between SIM cards and questions? Let's explore this further by turning to the world of science, storytelling, and Socrates.

## Interrobangs and Science

Believe it or not, there's ample intriguing research to back up your *24* (or other mystery-show) addiction. Researcher George Loewenstein wrote an article entitled "The Psychology of Curiosity," in which he reviews and analyzes the past fifty years of research on the psychology of curiosity. After studying almost everything written on what keeps us interested and engaged, Lowenstein comes to a simple conclusion. Lowenstein sets forth the "Gap Theory," explaining that curiosity occurs when we sense a gap in knowledge. This gap, Loewenstein says, causes pain and pain causes us to seek out the answer. He applies this to communicators, explaining that most presenters tend to close gaps before they've opened them. One of the secrets of engaging communication is to create the mystery before giving the answers. Interrobang preaching at its best.

---

*Most communicators tend to close gaps before we have opened them.*

---

Robert Cialdini affirms the power of questions in creating mystery, and the effectiveness of mystery as a tool for learning. In his research, Cialdini found the formation of a mystery story to be the most powerful tool for engaging students with material. He says that while descriptions demand attention and (simple) questions demand answers, mystery demands explanation, which is what grabs the attention of hearers and pulls them into the material with riveted interest.[13] Basically, its *24*. Yep, that's it. You can pretty much sum up decades of in-depth scientific research by scores of PhD's in two words: Jack Bauer.

## Interrobangs and Storytelling

Lisa Cron tells the story of a writer who was walking through an airport. With only a few minutes to catch his flight, he ducked into a bookstore and decided to pick a book based on the very first sentence. After looking through a number of possibilities, he picked the winner. What was the sentence that grabbed his attention? "Joel Campbell, eleven years old at the time, began his descent into murder with a bus ride."[14]

Cron goes on to explain the choice was based entirely upon curiosity. She writes, "From the very first sentence, the reader must want to know what happens next." Cron says that we are always looking for the "why" which makes us want to know both what already happened and what will happen. She writes, "I've heard it said that … all stories … can be summed up in a single sentence—all is not as it seems."[15]

Annette Simmons agrees. She argues that all people have the talent to become great storytellers because everyone possesses "the one natural talent to become a wonderful storyteller—the talent of curiosity." And "curiosity," Simmons writes, "causes you to pay attention."[16] In his work, *Story Engineering*, Larry Brooks contends that one of the core competencies of effective storytelling is to engage the audience with the question, "What if?" Again, we see the powerful connection between story and discovery.[17]

Though Jesus was not writing a mystery novel, he was revealing a mystery. Jesus was combining story and question in a way that engaged the listener on a journey of discovery.[18]

---

*Though Jesus was not writing a mystery novel,*
*he was revealing a mystery.*
*Jesus was combining story and question in a way that engaged the*
*listener on a journey of discovery.*

---

## Interrobangs and Socrates

Many of the great communicators in history understood the interrobang-power of discovery. Take Socrates for instance. You may be familiar with the term, the "Socratic Method." *Sure, it's asking a bunch of questions, right?* Yes, that's certainly part of it. But there's more. Socrates didn't simply pass on information. He wanted students to arrive at conclusions themselves. In order to do this, Socrates used a methodology that he referred to as *elenchus*. Basically, *elenchus* has four main components:

1) The first layer of *elenchus* is accurate self-evaluation. This aspect is "to get people to pay attention to the welfare of their souls."[19]

2) The second component of *elenchus* is the role of teacher as midwife. Socrates believed that there was truth within the individual and that the role of the teacher was to serve as midwife in order to facilitate delivery.[20]

3) Third, the purpose of *elenchus* is to facilitate enthusiastic discovery.[21]

4) Fourth, *elenchus* is suspicious of truth by proposition, choosing rather to combine the art of questions with the power of story.[22]

Let's connect a couple of the dots of *elenchus*. The first and third components have to do with the role of the student and the second and fourth pertain primarily to the role of the teacher. So, as we combine the first and second, then the third and fourth within the dynamics of the teacher-student relationship, we find that *elenchus* is this:

1) The teacher asks questions to facilitate self-discovery.

2) The teacher tells stories to facilitate world-discovery.

Are you seeing a trend? Do you see how the Savior, science, storytellers and Socrates all utilize the combination of story and questions to lead people into a journey of enthusiastic discovery?

Remember, you were born to both live and tell a story.

And you were born to uncover and discover mystery.

We now add the second dimension to our method:

1st DIMENSION
What is the SIM Card?
(Tell the Story)


2nd DIMENSION
What is the Interrobang?
(Guide into Mystery)

Now let's examine how to walk people through the interrobang journey.

## CHAPTER SIX

# *INTERROBANG PREACHING PART 2: GUIDING OTHERS INTO THE MYSTERY*

"Preaching the Good News of Jesus Christ is the highest, holiest activity to which a man can give himself."
-Wil Sangster[1]

Kind words are like honey,
sweet to the soul and healthy
for the body.
Proverbs 16:24

**How to do Interrobang Preaching**

The application of this dimension may seem more elusive
than the use of the SIM card. Tell stories? I can do that. Show
images? Check. Re-sign metaphors? Perhaps that will require
more digging, but I can do that too. But mystery? Come on, do
you want to transform preachers into John Grisham novelists?
Do I preach with a Sherlock Holmes hat and magnifying glass?

To be honest, I wondered that myself. How will this work on Sunday mornings? But as I've discovered, the application is really quite simple.

Once you've found your SIM card, you then add a second layer to interrobang preaching. Think of it this way: if the SIM card is your *methodology*, this next dimension is your *process*. Interrobang preaching includes layering-in four simple elements with your SIM card.

1. Lead in discovery (The mystery in the story)

As you begin your sermon preparation and process of interacting with the Biblical story, there will likely be things in the text that don't make sense. I encourage you not to ignore them. With all of the items on our to-do list, it can be easy to skip over what we don't understand, and simply preach what we know. But what if the greatest truth God wants to reveal to you and your audience begins with a question?

The hallmark scripture verse of an interrobang preacher is found in John 16. Jesus is nearing the end of his earthly ministry. He has just spent the greater part of three years with a group of twelve disciples. That is a long time! If you've ever been on a missions trip or at a youth camp, you know that for better or worse, you get to know people pretty well after a week in close quarters. However, Jesus' ministry wasn't a ten-day missions trip. It was a 1095-day missions trip. During this time, the disciples heard Jesus preach to the masses and had access to behind-the-scenes instruction. They witnessed Jesus heal blind eyes and saw him bring dead children back to life. They had even preached and cast out demons themselves. You would think that if anyone knew about God, Christ, the scriptures, miracles, and ministry, it would be the disciples.

In John 16, Jesus makes an amazing statement. He tells the disciples, "There is *so much more* I want to tell you." Wow! Even after a three-year crash course taught by Jesus himself, there was "so much more." So how would the disciples discover all of this "more" to the mystery? Jesus continues, "When the Spirit comes, he will guide you into all truth."[2]

The Spirit is your tour guide in the interrobang discovery of Christ. The Spirit is always leaving clues, giving hints, and nudging you in the right direction. The Spirit is continually leading you further and further into a life of enthusiastic discovery. Ask yourself what in the passage of scripture initially doesn't make sense? Is there anything you don't understand? Is there a mystery to uncover? Chances are that the greatest revelation you discover will begin with something you didn't initially understand.

As you lean further into the question, into the mystery, into the interrobang, you will find that the Spirit will lead you, guiding you into all truth, because that is what Jesus promised. Believe it or not, according to Jesus, the Spirit is actually a better sermon-prep partner than if Jesus were with you in the flesh writing the sermon! ("It is better for you that I go away... .")

As the Spirit leads you further into the mystery, something amazing takes place. We see it transpire in Matthew 16. Jesus was in the region of Caesarea Philipi, and he paused to ask the disciples two questions. First he asked, "Who do people say the Son of Man is?" "Well," they replied, "some say John the Baptist, some say Elijah, and others say Jeremiah or one of the other prophets." Then Jesus proceeds to ask the second question, "But who do you say I am?"[3]

Read that last question again. "Who do you say I am?" Notice anything? Jesus is giving a hint. Remember the burning bush? Remember Moses' question to God? "Who shall I say sent me?" And what was God's answer? "Tell them I AM has sent you."[4] Now read Jesus' question again. "But who do you say *I am*?" Jesus is not only asking a question, he's giving the answer. In the question itself, Jesus is declaring he is the Messiah. He is God. He is Immanuel, God with us.[5] The answer is within the mystery. The revelation is within the question.

This same type of discovery can occur in your sermon prep. As you allow the Spirit to guide you deeper into the mystery, he will give you greater revelation. You will move from preaching information to preaching revelation.

---

*"Christianity's first word is one of revelation.*
*It's last word is that of mystery."*
*-Leonard Sweet*

---

Also, when you are preaching on Sunday, don't jump straight to the answer. Start with the question. Share with your congregation some of the process of how something in the Biblical story didn't make sense initially. Ask the questions out loud on Sunday that you were asking in your sermon prep on Tuesday. Walk the congregation through some of the interrobang-journey the Spirit led you on that week.

And explain that the same Spirit is available to reveal truths in God's word to them. Too many people are questioning their faith when they should be discovering their faith. The Bible is more mystery novel than encyclopedia. When you (re)sign the metaphor of Scripture, you open up a whole new world of Spirit-led discovery into the mystery of Christ. Teach and equip your people to step into an interrobang journey of enthusiastic discovery with Jesus.

---

*Too many people are questioning their faith when they should be discovering their faith.*

---

2. Ask questions (The mystery within)

This is the simplest and most straightforward way to apply interrobang preaching in your messages: Stop periodically throughout your message to ask questions.

- If you're preaching on fear ask, "What is the greatest fear you are facing right now?"

- If you're preaching on dreams ask, "What would you do in life if money were no object?"

- If you're preaching on marriage ask, "How would your spouse describe your marriage right now?"[6]

Do you see the power of a question? During a sermon, it's easy to sit in the audience and think of all the other people in your life who need to hear what the preacher's saying. After all, if all those other people could just get their lives together, then it would be a lot easier for the rest of us! Questions cut to the heart of each individual. "Hey you. Yeah, you. Not your spouse. Not your kids. Not your neighbor two doors down. You. What is causing the fear in *your* life?" Questions have a way of forcing us to confront inner realities about our beliefs, attitudes, and actions.

---

*Questions have a way of forcing us to confront inner realities about our beliefs, attitudes, and actions.*

---

The temptation can be that it seems too obvious. Won't people automatically ask themselves these questions? Won't they automatically apply your message to their lives? The answer is a resounding, "no." We usually avoid asking ourselves tough questions. Want proof? When was the last time, as a preacher, you listened to a sermon and paused when taking notes to write down a question for yourself? Exactly. If you don't, your audience doesn't either. You need to ask them questions.

## Points as Questions

You might consider framing your supporting points as questions. I saw this done recently by speaker and author Alicia Britt Chole, and it was powerful. Alicia is a soft-spoken, gentle soul who reminded me of a cross between flower child and school teacher. When I heard Alicia, her audience consisted mostly of high-octane, highly motivated male leaders who were more likely to spend their free time in the woods with a rifle slung over their shoulders, or driving the lane on a basketball court, than running through a field of wild flowers. So when Alicia rose to speak, I was skeptical as to her ability to connect. Ten minutes into her talk, my heart was pierced (along with the other macho-dudes in the room.) Part of the power of her talk was in her questions. They were as follows:

1) Are you bowing to the idol of uniqueness? (Do you think that you have to be either the first to do something or the best at it for it to count?)

2) Do you possess the strength to be nothing?
3) Is your core well-watered?
4) Am I living in the singular or in the plural? (Am I living in my own strength or through the strength of the Holy Spirit)?

Alicia could have phrased these as statements.

1) Don't bow to the idol of uniqueness.
2) Possess the strength to be nothing.
3) Water your core.
4) Live in the plural.

While the talk would have still been strong, it wouldn't have possessed the soul-searching power that it did with the phrasing of questions. They forced us to look inward. They forced us to examine our hearts and our motives. They forced us to dig into the uncomfortable places in our lives where the answers aren't always nice and pretty.

Following the session, someone described Alicia as a kind and loving kindergarten teacher who repeatedly punched you in the throat while smiling at you! It was true. Our hearts were filleted. This group of energetic, Type-A, let's-get-something-done guys were all ready to sign up for two weeks of prayer and reflection at a local monastery! All because of the power of questions.

3. Press Pause (The mystery in the gap)

Admittedly, this may be the most difficult part of interrobang preaching to incorporate into a sermon. As we've mentioned before, not all of us are John Grisham. Not all of us are skilled at weaving together a mystery-narrative into our message that will have people on the edge of their seats, let alone leaving service to set their life-DVR for the next episode so they'll know how the cliffhanger resolves. But there is a simple step we can take to incorporate mystery into our SIM card.

Here it is: press pause. Begin with your SIM card, then press pause, and close with the ending of your SIM card. A summer intern, David, told me about something he heard from a professor: "A good sermon is a really good introduction, a really good conclusion, and not too much in between." There's probably some truth to this. What if we could take our SIM card, break it in two, and take advantage of the Gap Theory to engage people's interest?

My friend David Hertwick did this beautifully in a recent presentation on discipling youth. David made the point that in discipleship, we get what we measure, so it's important how we keep score. He told the story of his daughter playing soccer. (David showed a picture of his daughter as he was telling the story), and explained that the league his daughter played in didn't keep score. He also explained that he's a pretty competitive guy who loves soccer, so he kept score in his head. After the game, he would ask his daughter what the score was and each time her answer was vastly different than the actual outcome.

Having drawn us in with this story, David proceeded with his presentation, explaining how we measure success (keeping score) in discipleship matters greatly. Among youth, are we simply measuring their behavior or does the measure go deeper than this? Are we truly presenting the gospel to teenagers?

At the close of his talk, David went back to the story of his daughter. He explained that because he was such a big soccer fan, he was embarrassed his little girl didn't know the correct score. "Besides," David quipped, "We're Asian, so my kid should be good at math!" When he dug in a bit more, asking his daughter about the score, he discovered she was giving the team a point every time the goalie stopped the ball. As she was talking, the light bulb went on. David realized that when the goalie stopped the ball, people cheered. His daughter equated cheers with points. David ended by challenging youth pastors to cheer for the right things in student's lives, because what you cheer for is how they keep score.

David began with a SIM card. Then he pressed pause. And then he closed with the SIM card.

4. Preach Jesus (The mystery of Christ)

I know. You're wondering why you paid for a book to hear that the "secret" of great preaching is preaching Jesus. But in interrobang preaching, the secret to engaging your audience with wide-eyed wonder is simply that: preaching Jesus. Lest you be tempted to skip this section (or be done with the book!), don't. I thought I was preaching Jesus and wasn't. You may not be preaching Jesus either.

If you're a pastor, you probably feel the weight of coming up with new and creative messages each week. What is the new insight, the next great story or illustration, the next tweet-able statement that gets ten favorites and five retweets, or the next engaging video clip that makes people say "Wow, I never saw that spiritual truth in Monster's University before!" Our people are entertained on a daily basis—by people with loads more money than we have. Hollywood has access to the best equipment and technology and personnel. (Ever watched the credits and seen how many people it takes to pull off a short cartoon of prehistoric squirrel chasing an acorn?) In an entertainment-saturated environment, we feel the pressure to compete, to entertain, to be new and fresh and creative. Sunday passes and we immediately feel the weight of the next Sunday coming. It can be draining.

As I was feeling the pressure to engage Scripture in new ways, to find new insights and angles, the Holy Spirit dealt with me, reminding me of the simplicity of preaching Jesus. As I spoke one Sunday morning about the cross, the Holy Spirit nudged me, "Doug, when was the last time you did that? When was the last time you simply preached the crucified and resurrected Christ?" (Oh and by the way, you don't get to count Easter.)

Judah Smith, pastor of City Church in Seattle, tells this story: When he comes home from long trips, his youngest daughter always wants to "help" with the luggage. So she proceeds to "assist," leaving Judah not only carrying the weight of the bags, but navigating how not to trip over his daughter in the process. Judah talks about our desire to "help out Jesus" in our preaching and asks the simple question, "What if we let the gospel do the heavy lifting?"

After ten years of serving as his father's youth pastor, Judah's dad passed away from cancer and he inherited a five-thousand member church. Nine months into being the Lead Pastor and carrying the weight of coming up with something new and entertaining every week, he finally told the congregation: "I'm going to preach Jesus. Either the gospel works or it doesn't. If the gospel doesn't work, this church isn't going to work."

From Genesis to Revelation, the Bible is one story—the story of Jesus. Although we know this, sometimes we forget. For a great reminder, I highly recommend reading a kids' book: *The Jesus Storybook Bible.*[7] It is a wonderful and beautiful reminder of the story of the whole of scripture.

## From "Memorize This" to "Discover This"

As preachers, however, our training isn't in mystery. Our training is mostly in giving answers. So we structure the sentences of our sermons with periods instead of interrobangs. We feel the pressure that our sermons should provide every answer rather than fuel enthusiastic discovery. Perhaps too many times our preaching has led to "memorize this" instead of "discover this."

---

*Perhaps too many times the goal of our preaching has been "memorize this" instead of "discover this."*

---

Jesus didn't do that. Not all the time, at least. As often as Jesus gave answers, he led people into mystery.[8] We can too. Our preaching can be interrobang preaching. Our preaching should be interrobang preaching. Our preaching has the potential to lead people into the most enthusiastic discovery of their lives.

1st DIMENSION
What is the SIM Card?
(Tell the Story)

2nd DIMENSION
What is the Interrobang?
(Guide into Mystery)

- What questions do I have about the Biblical story?
- What questions can I ask that cause self-examination?
- Can I "split up" one of my stories to create a gap in knowledge?
- Where is Jesus in this message?

3rd DIMENSION- DYNAMIC
What is the Spirit Doing and
How Can We Respond?
Bring to Encounter

# CHAPTER SEVEN

## *BECOMING A SPIRITUAL SURFER*

"If there is no power it is not preaching. True
preaching, after all, is God acting."
-D. Martyn Lloyd-Jones[1]

The words of the godly are a life-giving fountain.
Proverbs10:11

### Becoming Spiritual Surfers

Growing up, I was fascinated with the ocean and with
surfing. I love sand and palm trees and water and often found
myself daydreaming of being at the beach with surfboard in
hand. The problem? I grew up in Northwest Pennsylvania.
While I loved my childhood, our local swimming hole was a
creek dammed up by a pile of rocks and, while fun to swim in,
did little to further my surfing career.

When my dad brought home a brochure about Southeastern
College, located in Lakeland, Florida, I felt an immediate

"prompting" to go to school there. For the first three years of my undergrad experience, both my lack of time and lack of owning a surfboard prevented me from learning the sport of my childhood dreams. But my senior year was different. I had worked extremely hard my first three and a half years in college, which left my final semester for three classes: a super-fun youth ministry class, introduction to computers (translation/ confession: using this newly-available thing called "the internet" to check Sportscenter), and Basic College Math I (pretty much the college version of addition and subtraction). I had the dream schedule which translated into increased beach time.

There was one problem, however. I'd broken my wrist during an intramural basketball game. While I wish the story involved me soaring above the rim and slamming the ball through the basket with such authority that it broke a bone, the truth is, I was running back on defense with nobody around me and tripped over my own two feet. The result of the injury was a blue cast that stretched from mid-hand to above my elbow.

I had waited a lifetime to make my surfing dreams come true. I couldn't let this inconvenience keep me and my new QuietFlight surfboard apart. My brother Steve, my friend Kevin, and I would drive to our favorite surf spot: second light at Cocoa Beach. As we neared Cocoa on the Bee-Line Expressway, I would make Kevin climb into the back seat and wrap my arm with a garbage bag and duct tape so I could get in the water. But alas, I quickly learned that I was no Soul Surfer. I needed both arms.

Years later at another break called S-Turns, in front of the now-famous beach house from *Nights in Rodanthe* in the Outer Banks of North Carolina, I caught my first real wave. I will never forget it. Previously, I'd ridden some smaller waves, but nothing like this. Sitting on my board in the ocean as the sun glistened off the water, I saw the wave coming. I paddled, popped up, and rode down the face of the emerald curl of water. It was one of the most amazing experiences of my life.

What I've since learned about surfing and the dynamics of a wave is that three elements are at play: the wind, the water, and the landscape. While there are different kinds of breaks (point breaks, beach breaks, and reef breaks), the basic components are the same. A wave occurs when the wind pushes the water over the landscape. Whether it is the sand on the bottom of a point or beach break, or coral at the bottom of a reef break, when the wind pushes the water over this surface, a wave is formed. A surfer's goal is to position him or herself where those three elements intersect. That's where the ride is beautiful, magical, and transformational.

And that is exactly our goal as preachers of the gospel. We want to be spiritual surfers. Where do spiritual surfers catch the best waves? Where the wind of the Holy Spirit pushes the water of the gospel over the landscape of culture.[2]

> *As a spiritual surfer, your goal is to position yourself*
> *where the wind of the Spirit pushes the water of the gospel*
> *over the landscape of culture.*

What could be more "interrobang" than this? What could be more "What if …?" What could lead to more "enthusiastic discovery" than riding the wave of the Spirit? At times our sermons can lean towards predictability. But the Spirit is always moving. The Spirit is continually doing something new and fresh and creative.

## Ocean Waves or Wave Pools?

Perhaps you've been to an amusement park with a wave pool. The scene probably looked something like this: tons of people who were hot and exhausted from standing in hour-long roller-coaster lines are now crammed into a pool dodging kids and yellow inner tubes. I'm not mad at wave pools. I suppose they are fine. But if you've been in a turquoise sea peering through the water at white sand, you know the difference.

I wonder if at times we've settled for wave pools, trying to manufacture our own waves rather than positioning ourselves as spiritual surfers in the wave of the Spirit? Which describes your preaching? Which describes your Sunday morning service? Wave pools or ocean waves?

## Are We Preaching from Jefferson Bible?

I have several different versions of the Bible in my office. Each year I usually change versions for my devotional reading to gain fresh perspective on scripture. One of the versions I have is the Jefferson Bible. But instead of serving as a translation for devotional reading, this version serves as a blatant reminder of what *not* to do with scripture.

I obtained my copy of the Jefferson Bible through the Smithsonian. (No, this story doesn't turn into a Nicolas Cage movie.) I ordered a replica from their online catalogue. The story of the Jefferson Bible is this: Thomas Jefferson liked the morals of scripture, but he didn't like the supernatural elements. So he cut and pasted texts—literally. Jefferson cut the miracles out of his Bible and discarded them, then took the portions containing moral teachings and pasted them back together. Thus, the Jefferson Bible. I've seen quite a few translations of scripture in the local Bible book store, but I've never seen a "cut and paste" version complete with scissors and white-out.

Theologically, the whole idea is appalling. As preachers of the gospel, we would never cut out the portions of scripture we don't like, or that contain hard teachings. We're much too spiritual and well-trained to do that. Instead, we cut and paste with our preaching. By not preaching for and offering people a chance to have a supernatural encounter with Christ and by failing to pray and believe for the miraculous in our corporate worship gatherings, we might as well be preaching out of the Jefferson Bible.

---

*By not preaching for the miraculous, we might as well be preaching out of the Jefferson Bible.*

---

I don't want to do that. I'm sure you don't want to do that either. So how do we preach the fullness of scripture including an expectation for healing, deliverance, and miracles?

## Jesus was a Surfer

Jesus was the ultimate spiritual surfer. (I'm also convinced he'd be a great natural surfer and thus my goal of surfing with Jesus on the new earth someday.) We have shown that Jesus used a lot of SIM cards and asked a lot of questions, but even those two elements fall short of how many times Jesus utilized this final piece of our renewed homiletic. Out of his 146 preaching encounters, Jesus used a supernatural demonstration and/or some type of call to participate in what the Spirit was doing 118 times. That's eighty percent! Eight out of ten times Jesus preached the good news, there was a demonstration of the power of the Spirit and/or a call for people to participate in what God was doing. Jesus not only caught the wave, he got barreled.

To see exactly what Jesus was doing, let's take a look at a series of miracles in the book of John. The first is a word of knowledge given to the woman at the well. The second is a healing of an official's son. The third is the healing of a crippled man at the Pool of Bethesda.

The religious leaders are not happy. Accusations are thrown at Jesus. While Jesus often doesn't answer such accusations, this episode is unique. Jesus actually answers. In doing so, he gives us a behind-the-scenes glimpse into how he operates in the miraculous. Furthermore, his answer serves as a template that not only explains these particular miracles, but all of his miracles in general.[3] In Jesus' explanation, three statements are particularly telling:

1) "My Father is always at his work to this very day, and I too am working."[4]
2) "Very truly I tell you, the Son can do nothing by himself; he can do only what he sees his Father doing, because whatever the Father does the Son also does. For the Father loves the Son and shows him all he does."[5]
3) "By myself I can do nothing; I judge only as I hear, and my judgment is just, for I seek not to please myself but him who sent me."[6]

These statements are momentous. First of all, Jesus reveals that although he is the Son of God, he doesn't perform miracles on his own. "By myself I can do nothing." So how is Jesus giving words of knowledge, speaking healing to children, and telling lame men to get up and walk? Empowered by the Holy

Spirit, he discerns the will of the Father, which brings people into an encounter with God. The result is that people weren't walking away from Jesus having encountered "lessons for today" or "thoughts to ponder," they left having encountered the Living God.

Throughout his life and ministry, Jesus was continually in the curl of the wave. He listened to the voice of the Spirit, ever-asking, "What is the Spirit doing and how can I respond?"

## Where Did We Lose Encounter?

Remember that pre-modern culture was based upon story and superstition. Modernity, in reaction to both, became extremely skeptical of personal experience and encounter, choosing to substitute "truth by story and experience" with "truth by proposition."[7] Not all scientists of modernity bought into this philosophy. For example, according to the work of British chemist and philosopher, Michael Polanyi, the type of thinking that elevates proposition and devalues experience is faulty at its core.

Polanyi begins his explanation with an analogy of a grandfather clock. He asks his reader to imagine a team of physicists and chemists who know everything there is to know about the inner-workings and mechanics of grandfather-clock technology, but who have never actually seen a grandfather clock. Watch them inspect every minute detail of the parts of the clock. They pore themselves over every spring and gear.

The results of such an endeavor, Polanyi explains, would be a group of scientists who can describe every particular detail, but don't know the pieces make a clock. In Polanyi's words, "The complete knowledge of a machine as an object tells us nothing about it as a machine."[8] In other words, knowing something through science alone is incomplete. To truly "know" something, you have to encounter it.

---

*In order to truly "know" something, you have to encounter it.*

---

Another example Polanyi uses is that of riding a bicycle. He's discovered from questioning engineers, physicists, and bicycle manufacturers, that none of them can fully explain the science of balance as it pertains to riding a bicycle. Think of it this way—in teaching a child to ride a bicycle, you can attempt to explain the principles of centrifugal and gravitational forces. You can show him or her that "for a given angle of unbalance the curvature of each winding [of the handlebars] is inversely proportional to the square of the speed at which the cyclist is proceeding."[9] (Try telling that to a five-year-old after you've just pulled the training wheels off of the bicycle. You're going to get two things: blank stares and skinned knees.) How does a child learn to ride a bicycle? By experience.

All of this leads Polanyi to conclude, "Science can then no longer hope to survive on an island of positive facts, around which the rest of man's intellectual heritage sinks to the status of subjective emotionalism."[10] For Polanyi, experience and encounter are not the enemy of science, but are a necessary part of truly being able to know any given thing.

---

*"Science can no longer hope to survive on an island of positive facts, around which the rest of man's intellectual heritage sinks to the status of subjective emotionalism."*
*-Michael Polanyi*

---

## Lessons from the (Global) South

As a converted Southerner (I converted to Jesus at five and to the South at twenty-five), I have learned many lessons from the great people of North Carolina. However, this lesson pertaining to the supernatural doesn't come from the American South, but from the Global South.

In his book, *The Next Christendom,* Philip Jenkins charts the explosive growth of the church in the Global South and predicts that in the years to come Christianity will continue to experience tremendous worldwide growth, a growth that will be "neither white nor European, nor Euro-American."[11] Jenkins proceeds to ask the question: to what should we attribute this explosive growth?[12] His findings attribute the growth to the supernatural.

Jenkins writes, "The Global South Christians retain a strong supernatural orientation" and notes that "often, Christianity grows and spreads in highly charismatic and Pentecostal forms."[13] He identifies the growth in these regions as mirroring the growth of the early church in the book of Acts—through preaching the gospel, casting out demons, demonstrating signs and wonders, healing the sick, and encountering the power of God.[14] Jenkins even goes on to say that the growth of Pentecostalism across the Global South is so astounding as to "justify claims of a new Reformation." He notes that it is not in the least unreasonable to identify Pentecostalism as "the most successful social movement of the past century."[15] Jenkins concludes, "For the foreseeable future … the dominant theological tone of emerging world Christianity is traditionalist, orthodox, and supernatural."[16] The Global Southerers understand encounter. They understand that people long for more than bullet points and "thoughts to consider." They understand that people long for an interrobang experience with God.

---

*People are longing for more than "thoughts to consider."*
*They are longing for an encounter with God.*

---

## These Stories are Our Stories

Scholar Robert Menzies provides what I consider to be the best summary of the theology of these renewalist groups that are experiencing explosive growth. Basically, Menzies says that the experience of signs and wonders can be traced to a central belief that characterizes such movements. The theological centerpiece is this: "these stories are our stories." When the Global Southerners and other renewalists groups read scripture, they are not merely reading a history lesson. They aren't simply trying to reconstruct the cultural and historical situation of the story in order to make a generalized application to life today. When they read a story in scripture, they see the story as their story. If God appeared to Moses in a burning bush, then he can appear to them. If God spoke to Mary in a dream, God can speak to them in a dream. If Jesus healed a paralyzed man, then he can heal today.

These stories are not simply distant accounts of what God did for someone else in some other land in some other time period. The stories live and breathe. The Spirit calls, inviting us to read these stories not merely for information, but for participation. He invites us into the narrative not as a casual observer, but as an action-seeking character. "Once upon a time in a land far, far away" becomes "right here, right now."

Notice the connection between SIM card and surfer. As you tell the story, you are inviting the audience to enter the water and ride the wave. The same God who tore down the walls of Jericho invites you to live that story today. The "curl-of-the-wave" moment may be that God will break down impossible barriers in the lives of people that very morning.

When I go the movies, especially action-adventure movies, I find myself wanting to be a particular character. As I see the hero driving a motorcycle at a high rate of speed through the crowded streets of Paris, taking out fifteen bad guys along the way, the adrenaline kicks in and I want to buy a motorcycle, move to Europe, and join the CIA. That is the power of story. It beckons us to want to be involved. But when I leave the theater, there has been no life-transformation. While I may have been entertained or inspired, the story stays on the screen. I'm no more a rogue CIA agent when I walk out of the theater than when I walked into it. The only difference in my life is that my hands are greasy from buttered popcorn. The amazing thing about the stories of scripture is they call for participation. You enter the story and can experience the very same things that David did, that Joseph did, that Esther did, that Peter did. The invitation of the Spirit is "these stories are your stories!"

Remember, you were born to both live and tell a story.

You were born to uncover and discover a mystery.

And you were born to encounter life and encounter Jesus.

Again, let's review our model:

1st DIMENSION
What is the SIM Card?
(Tell the Story)

2nd DIMENSION
What is the Interrobang?
(Guide into Mystery)

- What questions do I have about the Biblical story?
- What questions can I ask that will cause self-examination?
- Can I "split up" one of my stories to create a gap in knowledge?
- Where is Jesus in this message?

3rd DIMENSION
What is the Spirit doing and how can we respond?
(Bring to Encounter)

Let's continue by diving in and discovering practical ways to become a spiritual surfer.

# CHAPTER EIGHT

# *HOW TO PREACH AS A SPIRITUAL SURFER*

"Preaching is theology coming through
a man who is on fire."
-D. Martyn Lloyd-Jones[1]

The words of the godly encourage many.
Proverbs 10:21

## How to Preach as a Spiritual Surfer

No doubt preaching for the miraculous can be the most intimidating part of interrobang preaching. Even if you are the world's worst natural storyteller, coming up with a SIM card is easier than putting a guy's ear back on. But remember, God isn't necessarily asking you to put a guy's ear back on (unless you've had a particularly nasty board meeting and it needs to be done). God simply wants you to ask the question: What is the Spirit doing and how can we respond? Sometimes that might be offering a call for salvation. Other times it might be calling people forward for healing. Still other times it might be praying with people for supernatural empowerment to share Christ with others. Although the following is not an exclusive list, here are eight suggestions on how to preach as a spiritual surfer.

## 1. Preach for Encounter (The Face of God)

Recently I was privileged to hear from the fifth ranking member of the U.S. House of Representatives, Congressman James Lankford from Oklahoma. Part of Congressman Lankford's fascinating story is that prior to serving in Washington, he ran a youth camp. With 5000 students attending per week, and with an estimated ten percent of the entire population of Oklahoma having been to this camp, it was no ordinary youth camp. We met with the congressman in a small-group setting. After he shared his story, we had the opportunity to ask questions. Since I help run youth camps, I asked him to speak to the importance of camp as it pertains to the spiritual development of the next generation. The Congressman answered, "You know, it has been my experience that kids come to camp for two reasons. First, they are going to be at a place for an entire week with a large number of people of the opposite sex. Second, they would get on the bus and say something to the effect of, 'I hear people meet God there. I wonder if that's true?'"

Wow. Wouldn't that be a great thing for people to say about your church? Not necessarily, "I heard there's a great preacher there," although I hope there is. Not, "I heard the music is tremendous there," although that would be great too. But, "I heard people meet God there. I wonder if that's true?"

The story of Jacob at Bethel provides us with a great theology for this type of question—a theology of encounter. Jacob was traveling and the sun had gone down. He decided to stop for the night to sleep. He lay down and grabbed a rock for a pillow. It is there he encountered Yahweh in a dream and discovered his destiny. Jacob responded by building an altar and committing fully to the Lord. The Bible describes the event by saying, "There at Bethel he met God face to face, and God spoke to him."[2] Simply put, "Bethels" are places we go to meet God.

Some further aspects of Bethels are found Jacob's encounters in Genesis 28 and 35. Bethels are:

1) A Place of Revelation (Gen 28:13; 35:7b)
2) A Place Where You Lay Down All that Holds You Back (Gen. 35:2)
3) A Place of Promise, Calling, and Destiny (Gen. 28:13c-15; 35:11-12)
4) A Place of Name Change and Identity (Gen 35:10)
5) A Place Where You Build Altars (Gen. 28:18; 35:14)
6) A Place of Giving (28:22b; 35:14b)
7) A Place of Commitment (Gen. 28:20-21)

I've got more than a few years of ministry experience under my belt. I fully understand that not every Sunday morning is a "youth camp" service, nor should it be. Not every sermon is a home run. (There have been times when I preached "bunt singles" at best!) Not every altar call feels powerful. Yet the over-arching principle remains: what if Sunday mornings were Bethels? What if the ultimate goal is for people to say, "I heard people meet God here. I wonder if that's true?"

Pastors, we don't do services. We do Bethels. We're not service planners. We're Bethel architects. The "curl-of-the-wave" goal of our messages should not primarily be that people leave having learned more information, but having encountered Jesus Christ.

---

*"Bethels" are places you go to meet God.*
*We're not service planners, we're Bethel Architects.*

---

## 2. Preach Revelation

According to Jewish tradition, there are four levels of insight into the scriptures:

1) *Pshat* - This is the literal and simple interpretation. (Think morning devotional reading with a Study Bible.)
2) *Remez* - This is the more complex meaning, which includes studies of well-known rabbis in the Talmud.

(Think hermeneutical and exegetical study with commentaries and word studies.)

3) *Derash* - This includes metaphorical meaning.
4) *Sod* - This is the deepest and most spiritual level, in which the mysteries of Truth and the meanings of metaphors, parables, and mysteries are understood in levels that would touch the innermost reaches of the heart and mind. This is as much transformational as informational.[3]

Preaching *sod* is what interrobang preaching is all about. Look closely at the components of *sod*: metaphors and parables (SIM card), mysteries (interrobang), and transformation (what is the Spirit doing and how can we respond?)

I'm not against *remez*, but some training on preaching stops there. It shows us how to access commentaries, Bible dictionaries, and word studies, but doesn't show us how to access the throne of Almighty God. If our sermons are overflowing from commentaries, they make nice Bible studies, but if they're overflowing from our prayer life, they are revelation that brings people into a life-transforming encounter with Christ.

---

*If our sermons are overflow from commentaries, they are nice Bible studies, but if they are overflow from our prayer life, they are revelation that brings people into a life-transforming encounter with Christ.*

---

3. Preach the Risen Christ

On the first Easter morning, Mary Magdalene and the other Mary went to Jesus' tomb. When they arrived, they had an unexpected encounter with an angel who said to them, "He is not here. He has risen."[4] Unfortunately, this pattern continues as people still try to look for Jesus where he isn't. As central as the cross is to our doctrine and our faith, Jesus is not on the cross. Nor is he still in the tomb. Our Savior is risen and, having defeated all powers of death and darkness, is seated at the right hand of the Father. Jesus is alive and living in victory. In Ephesians, we are told that the very same power that raised Christ from the dead is available to us.[5] We must preach Christ risen and victorious.

*Yes, but what about suffering? What about times of trial and hardship?* I agree. We cannot ignore there are times when we walk through hardships. However, the Israelites turned an 11-day journey into a 40-year way of life. We must not mistake what God asks us to walk through for the destiny we're called to live in. Daniel walked through the lion's den, but he didn't live in the lion's den. David walked through the battle with Goliath, but he didn't live in the battle with Goliath. Shadrach, Meshach, and Abednigo walked through the fiery furnace, but they didn't live in the fiery furnace. Likewise, while we walk through times of trial and temptation, those trials are not our ultimate destiny.

---

*The Israelites turned an 11-day journey into a 40-year way of life. We must not mistake what God asks us to walk through for the destiny we're called to live in.*

---

For the first thousand years of the church, the predominant theology was *Christus Victor:* Christ is risen and has defeated all powers of death and darkness, and we are called to live out the victory of Christ.[6] It is time to reclaim our rightful heritage, position, and message of the good news of the risen Christ.

## 4. Preach with *Predoración*

I don't remember doing this, but my former worship leader tells me I did. I have to confess, I believe him. One time during the middle of an altar call, I swung around, looked at him, said, "You guys are killing me!" then continued with the altar call. Now preachers, don't judge. You have had those moments when the musicians weren't "flowing" with you too!

I was in Cuba recently and eating lunch with a local pastor. I commented on his worship team's amazing ability to flow with the Spirit and speaker, and to communicate that through music. I asked him how they did this. His response was two-fold. First, he said that they have a school of music and spend many hours in practice. Second, he said, "In Cuba, we have a concept: preaching is not one thing and worship another."

I'm convinced that our preaching needs what the Cubans have: something I have termed *predoración*. What is predoración? *Predicar* is Spanish for preaching and *adoración* is Spanish for worship. In the American church, we've separated the two. The Cubans understand that they flow together. They weave together prayer, exhortation, and worship in a way that brings forth a beautiful dance of Spirit, word, and response. You don't attend a Cuban worship service; you encounter a Cuban worship service.

To speak to a generation who says, "If I experience it, I will believe it," we must turn preaching from "thoughts for today" into an encounter with Christ. One way is by learning from the Cubans and preaching with predoración. In order to do this, we first must grasp the philosophy that preaching and worship are not separate. Secondly, we must practice. That's right, practice.

I was giving a brief message to a group of students recently and I connected with the worship team beforehand. I had them play behind me and then walked through with them what I sensed the Spirit was saying. We practiced how it would flow musically—what chords felt right and when and how they would build. What followed is that we led a group of students in a powerful time of prayer for unconfessed sin, filling of the Spirit, and prayer for each other, all in a brief amount of time.

*But that's not spiritual! You need to flow with the Spirit spontaneously.* I would respond by saying Peyton Manning is the best "flow-with-the-Spirit" quarterback ever. (In the NFL, it's called "calling an audible.") How can he do that? Because he prepares like nobody else. Peyton can make on-the-fly changes at the line of scrimmage because he has spent hours in the film room and on the practice field. Great "flow" moments are sometimes the result of great prepare moments. If the Spirit can speak to you in the midst of giving an invitation for response, certainly he is capable of speaking to you beforehand as well.

---

*Great "flow-in-the-Spirit" moments come out of great prepare moments.*

---

*But isn't that manipulation? Aren't you using music to manipulate people's emotions?* I suppose any communication technique could be used to manipulate if the heart of the preacher is to that end. With a pure heart before the Lord, we are simply utilizing the combination of worship and word to lead people into the curl of the wave. You would be upset with your worship team if they didn't practice. Preachers should certainly go over our material as well. Then what is wrong or manipulative about going over the material together? Besides, it's Biblical. When Elisha was preparing to bring the word of the Lord to Jehoshaphat, he first called for the musicians.[7] It may be the first instance of the preacher calling for the worship team before beginning the altar call!

By the way, don't feel as though you have to wait for the close of your message to bring the musicians on stage. Predoración can be done throughout your message as well. The African American church understands this. (Think black-gospel preacher with a Hammond organ in the background.) Of course you'll want the style of music to fit with your personality, zip code, and flow of the message, but the principle remains true. Music throughout the message encourages engagement and response. (Some young preachers of thriving churches are re-discovering this. Pastor Steven Furtick of Elevation Church periodically uses organ music behind him as he preaches.)

Preachers, get your worship team together. Practice reading scripture with them playing behind you. Feel, sense, and flow. Talk about when they need to build and pull back, when you want drums and when you don't. Then practice predoración as a part of your worship services and lead people to encounter God.

## 5. Preach with Announcement

In recent years, the trend in communication, whether in the pulpit, the classroom, or the boardroom, has placed less and less value on the communicator. Phrases such as "talking head" and "sage on the stage" are used—and not in a flattering manner. The emphasis has moved to "having a conversation." While I can understand and appreciate the need for greater dialog and audience feedback, as preachers we must not forget the power of prophetic proclamation.

Jesus certainly had conversations, such as with the woman at the well. There were also times when he was the conversation. Matthew records a summary of Jesus' ministry in the region of Galilee: "Jesus traveled throughout the region of Galilee, teaching in the synagogues and announcing the Good news about the kingdom. And he healed every kind of disease."[8] Matthew tells us that there were three aspects at work: teaching about the kingdom, demonstrating the kingdom, and announcing the kingdom.

In a world of conversation and dialogue, we must not lose the power of announcement. Periodically, as you weave throughout your master SIM card, you can move into "announcement" mode.

What do you announce? Here is where preachers get confused and where the power of announcement has gotten a bad name. We are not called to announce our opinions or political ideas or yell at people's sin. We are, however, called to announce two important aspects of the kingdom:

1) Announce the "I AM"

Something powerful happens when we begin to announce who God is. Announce God's power. Announce God's love. Announce God's mercy and grace and forgiveness. Announce God's power to heal and restore. Announce that he is our protector, provider, deliverer, savior, healer, baptizer, and soon-and-coming King. Announce that he is the great I AM.

## 2) Announce who "We Are"

Something equally powerful takes place when we begin to announce who we are. The voices in people's heads are constantly at work telling them they're not good enough: they are failures, they are going to be defined by their mistakes, they are slaves. When we announce who people are in Christ, the announcement begins to break those thought patterns and replace them with the truth of what God says about us. We are forgiven. We are redeemed. We are bought with a price. We are destined. We are sons and daughters. Because of the I AM, we are! Don't be afraid or ashamed to boldly and passionately proclaim and announce these important aspects of the Kingdom.

## 6. Preach for the Miraculous

It is important to both preach for and create space for the miraculous. First, we cannot cut and paste. We must put down our scissors and preach the passages we don't fully understand. We must preach the stories of Jesus multiplying loaves and fishes and healing blind eyes—and not just as spiritualized life lessons either. A message on a story where Jesus heals someone of paralysis cannot simply be a teaching on how we need to move past our emotional paralysis. That is a Jefferson-Bible translation.[9]

If we preach for the miraculous, we must also create space in our services where we pray for it as well. We cannot preach on healing and then say, "God bless you as you go. Walk in healing this week." Again, that is the Jefferson version. A sermon on healing should include prayer for healing.

---

*A sermon on healing should include prayer for healing.*

---

As someone who has grown up largely in charismatic circles, I've seen the spectrum: I've seen the real. I've seen they hype. I've seen the failure. I've been in services where physical healings have taken place before my eyes. I've been in services that seemed so emotionally hyped and fake it made me angry. And I've experienced the pain of praying seven years for my mother to be healed of paralysis and not see that healing on this earth. As my friend and evangelist, Joe Phillips says, "I'm in sales. He's is management. When it comes to healing, I don't understand all of it, I just pray for all of it." It's not our job to heal. It's not our job to provide the financial miracle. It's not our job to bring the marriage back together. It is our job to preach the whole of scripture and to provide space in our services where people can receive the miraculous.

That isn't to say you must call people forward for prayer every week or end each message with an altar call. Remember, this is not about a single method or methodology, rather it's about ending each message inside of the curl of the wave. What is the Spirit doing and how should we respond?

7. Preach to a Culture of Expectancy and Engagement

As someone who travels and preaches to different audiences, I've experienced an interesting occurrence: the same message preached by the same individual can have vastly different results. While there may be several factors at play, the most potent factor is the expectancy and receptivity of the audience. There is nothing like preaching to a receptive crowd. When the audience comes with an expectant spirit and when they are engaged in what the Spirit is doing in that service, the message often flows. In contrast, when you're looking out over a sea of bored expressions and crossed arms, there's a dampening effect on the message. There is so much more at play than the ego of the speaker. There is a spiritual dynamic at work, and it has to do with a culture of expectancy and engagement.

Samuel Chand offers a great metaphor for the power of culture. He says that if vision is the high-octane sports car, culture is the road.[10] You can have a Corvette with a turbo-charged 350 and the potential to cruise at 120 mph, but if you tried to run the car on a dirt road with rocks and ruts, the Corvette wouldn't perform. There is nothing wrong with the potential of the car; rather, the problem lies with the condition of the road.

Pastors, the car is your sermon. The road is the culture of expectancy and the engagement of your audience. Now before you get mad and start directing blame at your audience, and before you preach a message on how they're like the Israelites with stubborn hearts, look at your responsibility as a communicator and leader to help pave the road.

## Expectancy

First, teach people that their attitude of expectancy influences their capacity to receive blessing. The widow came with almost nothing. Down to her last bit of oil, she takes a step of faith and obedience, going from house to house, collecting jar upon jar, showing us that sometimes our level of preparation influences our level of expectation. This in turn increases our reception of what the Lord wants to give.

Teach your audience this principle. Teach them that every time the word of God is preached, the Lord is pouring out from heaven. The question is: Do we have the containers to receive? Teach them that simple things—like their posture, or coming ready with a notepad or iPad—demonstrates a heart that is expectant to receive from the Lord.

## Engagement

The second aspect of a well-paved road is teaching your people the importance of being engaged with the message. We desire people to be engaged in worship. In other words, we don't want them to simply stand there observing. We want them to participate. We want them to sing, to clap, to lift their hands. While we teach that worship is a participatory sport, we seem to view preaching as a spectator sport. The truth is, people need to engage with the message much the same as they engage in worship.

As the word of God is preached, the Spirit is trying to impact people's lives. The Spirit wants to encourage and strengthen them, and to increase their faith, joy, and peace. The Spirit is at work trying to move them from the mindset of slaves to the mindset of sons and daughters, and to open their eyes to the height and depth and vastness of the love and power of the risen Christ. But the Spirit can't do it alone. Our cooperation and engagement is needed.

One of the most powerful ways we can receive what the Spirit is doing in our lives is through the power of agreement. This is the power of the "amen." Perhaps you learned this version of an oft-quoted verse: "All God's promises are yes and amen." When the verse is translated this way, God's promises seem automatic. That's not what the verse says. The actual wording reads, "For no matter how many promises God has made, they are 'Yes' in Christ. And so through him the 'Amen' is spoken by us to the glory of God."[11]

According to Paul, there are three aspects to the promises of God. First, there is the God who makes the promise. Because God cannot and does not lie, the first part is set and good to go. Then, the promises are "yes" in Christ. Because Christ has already been crucified, resurrected, and is seated at the right hand of the Father, his part in the equation is complete as well. It's the third part that is the variable. For the promise to be made effective, the "Amen" must be spoken by us.

"Amen" means "so be it." In other words, the Spirit wants to deliver promises to us, but needs our cooperation and agreement. That's why when the word is preached, it's important for the audience to say "amen." It's not just an old-fashioned tradition or something to get the preacher fired up. As you say "amen," you are stepping into agreement with the promises the Spirit wants to deliver in your life. I don't think the Spirit is particular about the verbiage. If "amen" seems old-fashioned, express "that's good" or "yes." Just don't be a passive observer. Actively engage in what the Spirit wants to do in your life.

---

*As you say "amen," you are stepping into agreement with the promises the Spirit is trying to deliver in your life.*

---

Have you noticed that re-paving the stretch of road on your way to work doesn't happen overnight? It's usually a long process, filled with orange barrels and lane closures. In other words, it takes time and hard work. Once the new lane is open, you realize it was well worth the effort. Creating a culture of expectancy and engagement is not a one-time message. Rather, we must continually remind our audience of the importance of these dynamics. It requires time and effort. However, the word of the Lord will be received more smoothly as a result.

## 8. Preach with an Increased Anointing

Did you realize there are moments in your life when God can and will increase your anointing? It happened to Elisha. Elijah was nearing the end of his life and asked Elisha what he could do for him before he was taken to heaven. Elisha didn't hesitate. He responded by asking for a double portion of the Spirit. Keep in mind there were conditions in Elisha's life that made him a prime candidate for this increase in anointing. He followed the calling on his life with abandonment, burning his plow and oxen in a statement that there was no plan B. He faithfully served his mentor and walked under authority, being known as a man "who used to pour water on the hands of Elijah."[12] Thus, because Elisha followed and honored this man of God to the very end, and was there when Elijah was taken up to heaven in the chariot, Elisha did indeed inherit a double portion.

The increased anointing in Elisha's life was made manifest in at least ten different areas, one of them being an increased anointing for preaching. When King Jehoshaphat was seeking for a prophet of the Lord, Elisha was immediately identified with the statement: "The word of the Lord is with him."[13]

This is something I have experienced in my life as well. While preparing to teach a masters level course on preaching, I discovered that one of the people taking this course was Rich Wilkerson. In case you're not familiar with Pastor Rich, he is one of the top preachers in my tribe of the Assemblies of God. "Oh great," I thought "My first class as an instructor and who is sitting on the other side but Rich Wilkerson! God surely has a sense of humor." I told Pastor Rich before class that my teaching methodology was going to be, "So, Pastor Rich, what do you think about that?"

The class had a great week together learning many of the same principles I've shared in this book. At the week's conclusion, I felt prompted to do something a bit unusual. I taught on the principle of increased anointing, and then asked Pastor Rich and Dr. Bob Rhoden (the other instructor for the class and a father in the faith) to lay their hands on us and pray for increased anointing. Make no mistake, though I was one of the teachers of the class, I wasn't going to miss out on receiving from that prayer.

I'll never forget Pastor Rich laying his hands on me and praying for an increase in the anointing to preach. And it has made a difference. As I've preached since then, I've experienced not only an increase in anointing as I communicate God's word, but I've seen an increase in response as well.

Here is what I encourage you to do: Think of a spiritual mentor in your life, someone who carries an anointing to teach and preach. Go to him or her and ask for prayer. Ask the Lord to use him or her to increase anointing on your life.

Remember, you were born to both live and tell a story.

You were born to uncover and discover mystery.

You were born to encounter life and encounter Jesus.

One more time, let's review the dimensions of interrobang preaching:

1st DIMENSION
What is the SIM Card?
(Tell the Story)

2nd DIMENSION
What is the Interrobang?
(Guide into Mystery)

- What questions do I have about the Biblical story?
- What questions can I ask that will cause self-examination?
- Can I "split up" one of my stories to create a gap in knowledge?
- Where is Jesus in this message?

3rd DIMENSION
What is the Spirit doing and how can we respond?
(Bring to Encounter)

# CHAPTER NINE

## *PREACHING IN SPIRALS*

"In the sermon the foundation for a new world is laid.
Here the original word becomes audible."
- Dietrich Bonhoeffer[1]

"The preacher, who is the messenger of God,
is the real master of society; not elected by society to be its ruler, but elect of God to form its ide-
als and through them to guide and rule its life."
-Rev. Charles Silvester Horne, minister and
a member of British Parliament[2]

We're almost finished. But before we wrap up, I want to add one final dimension to your preaching by asking this question: What is God's favorite shape? Don't worry, I'm not leading you into a theological jungle with questions like: "Can God make a rock so large that He can't lift it?" I'm serious. What is God's favorite shape?

Even if you've never been asked that question, I bet you have an answer. Our supposed answer can be found in pulpits all across America on Sunday mornings. According to our preaching, God's favorite shape is a line. We start at point A and attempt to move people to Point B. We want to get as many people as possible from the beginning of the line to the next point on the line.

But what if God doesn't work in lines? What if we have overlaid our Western preference in geometric shapes on God? What if God's favorite shape is a circle? Before you conclude that I'm off my theological rocker, let me build my case.

According to scripture, the first shape God drew was a circle. Proverbs says,

When He established the heavens ...
he drew a circle in the face of the deep (Proverbs 8:27, ESV).

According to Solomon, the creation of the universe began with a circle. It makes sense when you think about it. What shape are the planets? What is the pattern of orbit of the planets? The universe doesn't move in lines. The universe moves in circles.

Once you understand this, you will begin to notice circles everywhere. Have you ever had a friendship you'd nearly forgotten about seemingly resurface out of nowhere? Circles. Have you ever thought you missed an opportunity, or nearly given up on a dream, only to be surprised by its sudden reappearance? Circles.

The Bible is also written in circles. It begins in Genesis with Adam and Eve in Paradise or (my translation) a wedding in a garden. According to Revelation 21-22, we are shown that it will re-begin with the marriage supper of the Lamb in what's described as a renewed Eden—another wedding in a garden. Even accounts in the Bible are written in circles. The story of Abraham and Isaac, as well as entire books of the Bible such as Numbers, are written in a genre known as ring composition.[3]

---

*The Bible begins with a wedding in a garden and it will re-begin with a wedding in a garden. It is one story throughout—the story of Jesus.*

---

To understand ring composition, think *Lord of the Rings*. Sam and Frodo begin in the Shire. From the Shire, they set about on their epic adventure and the "ending" has them re-beginning in the Shire. They are at the same place, but they are not the same people, and they have a new perspective.

When you preach, preach with God's favorite shape. Preach in spirals. Begin with your SIM card. Weave people through the SIM card with interrobang preaching. Then circle around to your original SIM card again. You will be at the same place, but having taken the journey, your audience will not be the same people or have the same perspective. It is at the end of the spiral that you become a spiritual surfer, asking the question, "What is the Spirit doing and how can we respond?"

## A Final Blessing

Fourteen years ago, I had a God-encounter in the front of the Concord First Assembly auditorium. (You can read the story in the Epilogue.) Since that time, the Spirit has led me further and further into this beautiful mystery of reclaiming my primary call to preach the gospel. I certainly don't have it all figured out. I have so much more to learn and discover. But it's a journey I wouldn't trade for the world.

One of my favorite things to do with my kids is to read them a bedtime story. Among our best loved are the works of Dr. Suess. He has many great stories, but my first choice is *Oh, The Places You'll Go!* As I read it to my kids, I dream dreams for their lives. I dream of how God will use them and think about the greatness of the calling upon their lives. I think of their future and destinies. I am reminded of our Heavenly Father who is dreaming great dreams for our lives as well—interrobang dreams.

I love the words of Theodore Geisel so much, in fact, that I've committed the final part of *Oh, The Places You'll Go!* to memory. I sometimes use it as a "blessing" over people when I speak. May you be blessed as you read these words. May your calling—your primary calling—to preach the gospel of Jesus Christ be unlocked within you and unleashed to the world.

Oh the places you'll go. There is fun to be done!
There are points to be scored. There are games to be won.
And the magical things you will do with that ball
will make you the winning-est winner of all.
Fame! You'll be famous as famous can be,
with the whole wide world watching you win on TV.

Except when you don't.
Because sometimes you won't.

I'm afraid that sometimes you'll play lonely games too.
Games you can't win
'cause you'll play against you.

All alone!
Whether you like it or not,
Alone is something you'll be quite a lot.

And when you're alone, there's a very good chance
You'll meet things that will scare you right out of your pants.
There are some, down the road between hither and yon,
That can scare you so much you won't want to go on.

But on you will go
though the weather be foul.
On you will go
though your enemies prowl.
On you will go
though the Hakken-Kraks howl.
Onward up many a frightening creek,
though your arms may be sore and your sneakers may leak.
On and on you will hike, and I know you'll hike far
and face up to your problems, wherever you are.

… So be sure where you step
… Be dextrous and deft
and never mix up your right foot with your left.

And will you succeed?
Yes! You will, indeed!
(98 and 3/4 percent guaranteed.)

Kid, you'll move mountains!

So be your name Buxbaum or Bixby or Bray
Or Mordecai Ali Van Allen O'Shea,
you're off to Great Places!
Today is your day!
Your mountain is waiting.
So get on your way!⁴

So go ahead, live and tell the story.

Uncover and discover the mystery.

Encounter life and encounter Jesus.

Live and preach with interrobang.

Connect with Doug

To book Doug for a speaking engagement, or to share what is resonating in you, connect with him at:

facebook.com/douglas.witherup

@douglaswitherup

douglaswitherup

dwitherup@ncag.org

# EPILOGUE:
## THE STORY OF A WANDERING PREACHER

Originally, I had included my story in the introductory chapter. As I re-read the manuscript one more time, I grew impatient. I found myself thinking, "Get to the point, Witherup!" So what was originally two introductory chapters became one, and several stories and sections were cut. Yet my story is a huge part of the back story of this book and I hope that by sharing it, it will serve as an encouragement to some who it may resonate with.

I was walking across the dimly lit auditorium of Concord First Assembly, where I served on staff, for no other reason than to take a short cut. I was on my way from the finance office back to my office and instead of going through the main hallway, I cut through the sanctuary. It was there that I had an unexpected encounter with someone that altered the course of my life and ministry. Before we get to exactly what happened in the front of the auditorium that day, allow me to bring you up to speed.

I was raised in a rural church in Northwest Pennsylvania. The church had a fairly large youth group of around fifty, and a great volunteer youth pastor and adult leaders. As a junior in high school, I attended my first youth convention in Pittsburgh. It was a gathering of thousands from across the state. I had never seen or experienced anything like it. The speaker for the weekend, Sam Rijfkogel (pronounced "Rife-kogel"), communicated with amazing humor, creativity, and anointing. I remember thinking at the time, "Wow, it would be really cool to do what Sam does."

A year later, I was on a missions trip to the Dominican Republic where I had a powerful and transformational encounter with the Lord. Several weeks after our return, we were at First Assembly in Erie, PA where Pastor Jim Grove preached a message on Isaiah's response to God: "Here am I, send me." When Pastor Jim gave the altar call that night, I couldn't reach the front fast enough. If anyone has ever begged his or her way into the ministry, it was me! God had so radically transformed my life that I couldn't imagine doing anything else except serve him.

A couple of weeks after this, I found myself in our family living room on our plaid brown couch watching a Billy Graham crusade on our dial television set. I'm not even sure I was watching it on purpose. It may have been the only thing worth watching on the three TV channels we got. As I watched the program, I had a strong sense God was calling me to preach.

And I spent the next seven years of my life avoiding that calling.

It's not what you think. I didn't run from God or from the ministry. I was done running. I loved Jesus and wanted to serve him. I went to Southeastern University to study for ministry and was involved in the drama team while I was there. I spent my summers ministering at youth camps. Immediately following Southeastern, God connected me with Pastor Joe Phillips, who brought me to Concord First Assembly where I ended up on staff. I wasn't running from God, nor was I running from a call to ministry. So what was I running from?

What I had let slide was my specific call to preach. It wasn't a calculated decision, mind you. Over the years I had taken small steps away from that calling. During my college years, I battled insecurity in my calling and lacked the courage to tell others of about it. I wasn't bold enough to tell my non-Christian friends that I was called to preach and even within the church, there didn't seem to be as much emphasis on young people with a call to preach. I saw plenty of people my age involved in ministries such as music and drama, but preaching didn't seem to be emphasized as much.

As I completed college with preaching already low on my priority list, the busyness of ministry delivered the final blow. I was serving in the youth department and found myself planning retreats, organizing missions trips, keeping track of the finances, hanging out with and discipling students, and trying to grow leaders. Preaching and sermon preparation slid further and further into the background. At least until the day I took a short-cut through the sanctuary at Concord First Assembly.

It was there that I "just happened" to run into Pastor Phil Bennett. Phil is a tall man with neatly combed silver hair, and is a combination of sage and spiritual guide— a modern-day St. Francis of Assisi. He is one of those people who seems to have a direct connection with God. In the moments that followed, Phil stopped me and, in his casual and gentle way, mentioned a few things he felt that God was sharing with him about my life. I stared in disbelief. Had he been reading my journal? Had he been spying on me? How did he know these things? (Even though I was raised in a Spirit-empowered tribe, I was at that point a bit skeptical concerning some of the gifts of the Spirit.) As Phil shared with me, I was wrecked. All it took was a few moments in the front of the sanctuary for God to remind me of my calling—my primary calling—to preach the gospel.

Others share this type of story as well. Pastor Russell Evans is founder and pastor of Planetshakers church in Melbourne, Australia. Planetshakers has grown to be a city-impacting church of 10,000, and the music of Planetshakers has impacted the lives of hundreds of thousands around the globe. Furthermore, Pastor Russell is a tremendous communicator who travels the world preaching with powerful revelation and insight.

It wasn't always this way. Russell tells of growing up as an extremely insecure pastor's kid. His insecurity was fueled in part by an English teacher. The teacher had assigned a book to which

Russell's parents objected, and out of anger and embarrassment, the teacher responded bitterly. The words "Russell cannot communicate verbally or in writing" were actually written on his school records.[1] Though the comment was later removed by the school principal, the seeds of discouragement had been deeply planted. Russell writes that although he felt a call to do something great for God, for years he chose to believe the lie of the enemy.

What is interesting is the nature of the attack. Pastor Russell is an outstanding leader, but the words were not attacking his leadership. He is a gifted musician, but the attack was not against his musical ability. The attack came specifically against his ability to communicate.

Perhaps this is no accident. This type of attack happened to the apostles in the midst of the catalytic growth of the early church. As the church experienced rapid multiplication, three attacks were leveled specifically at preaching.[2]

1) Direct Hit- The apostles were put into jail and, if it hadn't been for Gamaliel's intervention, probably would have been killed.

2) Discouragement- The apostles were flogged and warned not to teach or preach again.

3) Distraction- The apostles faced the temptation to allow preaching to become secondary to leadership and social justice issues.

Since the first days of the church, preaching and preachers have been targeted because the enemy recognizes them to be primary catalysts of growth for the church. As preaching great John Stott has said, "Not only has [the enemy] effectively silenced some preachers, but he has demoralized those who continue to preach."[3]

---

*Since the first days of the church, preaching and preachers have been targeted because the enemy recognizes them to be primary catalysts of growth for the church.*

---

Perhaps you share these stories. Well, maybe not these exact stories, but something along these lines. You know you're called to preach, but if you're honest, you'd admit preaching has slid to the background of your ministry. Perhaps there have been issues that have tried to take you out of ministry. Perhaps (either from internal or external voices), you have faced discouragement about your communication abilities. Perhaps the demands of ministry have squeezed out your sermon prep time, leaving you depleted and feeling that preaching has become another chore rather than a joy. If you resonate with this at all, you may be experiencing your "front-of-the-sanctuary" moment—meaning God is restoring to you to your primary calling.

# NOTES

*I realize that reading through footnotes may not be the most engaging of experiences. But as one of my doctoral cohorts once remarked about an author: "Their theology is in the footnotes." I encourage you to at least scan the notes for some additional resources and ideas which may spur further thought.*

Preface/ Introduction

[1] Andrew Blackwood in John Stott, *Between Two Worlds*, (Grand Rapids, MI: Eerdmans Publishing, 1982), 43.

[2] D. Martyn Lloyd-Jones *Preaching and Preachers* (Grand Rapids, MI: Zondervan, 2011), 31.

Chapter 1

[1] P.T. Forsyth in John Stott, *Between Two Worlds*, (Grand Rapids, MI: Eerdmans Publishing, 1982), 38.

[2] Keith Houston, *Shady Characters: The Secret Life of Punctuation, Symbols & Other Typographical Marks,* (New York, NY: W.W. Norton & Company, 2013). The term "interrobang" is formed from the Latin *interrogitio* ("question") and the English "bang," which was a slang word for an exclamation point.

[3] Luke 24:41, italics added.

[6] It could be argued that these numbers are not exact in the sense that one could potentially combine (or separate) some of the encounters, making the total number of preaching encounters a few more or less than 146. My approach was to follow as closely as possible the divisions made by the editors of the NIV Bible. I believe the broad picture they portray remains accurate. Also, in many instances Jesus utilized more than one method, which explains why the percentages add up to more than one hundred percent (Doug Witherup, Study of Jesus' Preaching Encounters, Unpublished Chart, 2011).

## Chapter 2

[1] John Stott, *Between Two Worlds*, (Grand Rapids, MI: Eerdmans Publishing, 1982), 36.

[2] Chip and Dan Heath, *Made to Stick,* 19-20.

[3] This is not to say that all of Jesus' parables contain every element of story, image, and metaphor, but rather to suggest that some do, and there is greater complexity to some of the parables than just a story. Robert Stein notes that many grew up with the definition of parable as "an earthly story with a heavenly meaning," but says that does not accurately convey the richness of Jesus' parables. He goes on to discuss the importance of metaphor in the parables (Stein, *The Method and Message of Jesus' Teachings*, 33-38). Theologian Brad Young, in his extensive work on the parables of Jesus, uses phrases such as "images of an illustration," "word-pictures," "vivid images," and "dynamic metaphors" to describe Jesus' parables. (Brad Young, *The Parables: Jewish Interpretation and Christian Interpretation* [Peabody, MA: Hendrickson Publishers], 1998), 3-4). In his homiletic text, *Giving Blood,* Leonard Sweet talks about the power of narrative metaphors, or what he calls "narriphors."

[4] Lisa Cron, *Wired for Story: The Writer's Guide to Using Brain Science to Hook Readers from the Very First Sentence* (Berkeley, CA: Ten Speed Press, 2012), 1.

[5] Cron, 2.

[6] Ibid.

[7] According to further research, story also appears to contribute to how we formulate our identities and interpret meaning to fit our world and circumstances. In his work, *Religion in Human Evolution,* Robert Bellah says that humans are experiencing a "crisis of incoherence." He explains how we strive to make meaning of the world through story and to find our meaning through our place in story. He goes on to explain the difference between D-cognition and B-cognition, wherein D-cognition is learning truth by proposition, and B-cognition is learning truth through experience, story, and symbols. Bellah asserts that without story and symbol, we lose our capacity to see our future and therefore become trapped. According to Bellah, we need B-cognition to give us what he refers to as "symbolic transcendence," to help us find our place in the story. Bellah is particularly critical of religious faith that attempts to communicate truth primarily through proposition. He writes, "To identify religion with a set of propositions whose truth can be argued would be to make it into what more accurately should be called philosophy." As he clearly articulates, "narrative is the heart of identity" (Bellah, *Religion in Human Evolution*, 34).

[8] Annette Simmons, *Whoever Tells the Best Story Wins* (New York, NY: AMACOM Books, 2007), 12. Hear that preachers? Not whoever crafts the best argument, nor whoever shouts the loudest. Whoever tells the best stories wins.

[9] Thomas Hobbes, "De Corpre," in *Body, Man, and Citizen,* ed. Richard S. Peters (New York: Collier, 1962); Quoted in Bellah, 39.

[10] Myth is used here to mean stories. Pre-modern cultures would pass on their heritage through stories, some of which were mythical. With the rise of modernity, stories came to all be lumped into the "myth" category and thus, rejected as primitive and superstitious. Fire didn't come about by a Greek god. Rather, there was a scientific explanation for fire. Thus, all stories got a bum rap. The assumption was story = mythology, proposition = truth.

[11] John Broadus, whose *On the Preparation and Delivery of Sermons* has been called "the primary homiletical textbook ... [of the] late nineteenth through mid-twentieth century," and whose influence on preaching is "difficult to exaggerate" says this: "What we call illustrations are used to explain, to prove, to adorn, to awaken the attention, arouse the feelings, and help the memory." He goes on to say, "strictly speaking, one would not call Illustration a distinct class of the materials of discourse," but instead a "means of adornment" (John Broadus, *A Treatise on the Preparation and Delivery of Sermons*, ed. Edwin C. Dargan [Birmingham, AL: Solid Ground Christian Books, 1870], 15).

[12] Ann Jurecic, author of *Illness as Narrative,* examines the effect of propositional versus narrative truth on those who are ill. She explains that with the emergence of the scientific method and subsequent scientific explanation of symptoms, diseases, prognosis, and treatment, stories began to vanish. However, Jurecic reports that these scientific (propositional truth) explanations have failed to connect with patients. Patients are not finding answers and meaning in medical journals; they are finding them in story. Patients are not asking for a bullet-point list, they are asking, "What's my story?" Jurecic writes, "This reflects the profound need people have to tell these stories in an era when religious and folk explanations no longer give satisfying and complete meaning to their experience, and where

biomedicine largely excludes the personal story" (Ann Jurecic, *Illness as Narrative* [Pittsburgh, PA: University of Pittsburgh Press, 2012], 11, 18). For Jurecic, humans not only crave story and narrative, they need it to find meaning and identity. The attempt to give people meaning and purpose through propositional statements simply does not work.

[13] The hesitancy to utilize images in propositionally-driven communication can again be traced to Plato, with theologians following suit. Timothy Gorringe has written on the relationship between theology and art. In his work, Gorringe states, "Plato was … hostile to images. Plato felt images tended to replace the original order of divine being with a man-made order of non-being. In that sense, images could be idolatrous, leading us to worship an imitation of the truth." Gorringe goes on to explain how Plato's philosophy affected the methodology of the church, saying that "Christian teachers drank deeply from this spring." Gorringe notes one example of theologian Clement of Alexandria writing that "when art flourished, error increased" (Timothy Gorringe, *Earthly Visions: Theology and the Challenges of Art* [New Haven, CT: Yale University Press, 2011], 25). Robin Jensen chronicles the history of art in early Christianity and agrees. She explains that early Christian thinkers and writers often linked art to idolatry and thus became skeptical of images (Robin M. Jensen, *Face to Face: Portraits of the Divine in Early Christianity* [Minneapolis, MN: Augsburg Fortress Press, 2005]).

[14] Lynell Burmark, *Visual Literacy* (Alexandria, VA: ASCD Publications, 2002), 5-10.

[15] In his work, *Beauty Will Save the World,* Gregory Wolfe argues for what he terms a "blessed symphony" of the four cultures of thinkers, prophets, humanitarians, and artists. He writes, "Public discourse has increasingly come to be dominated by warring academic elites" and says

that we need "non-academic artists and writers who balance a passion for truth and goodness with the concreteness that beauty demands." For Wolfe, the academics need the artists; propositions need images (Gregory Wolfe, *Beauty Will Save the World* [Wilmington, DE: ISI Books, 2011], xiii).

Chapter 3

[1] John Broadus, *A Treatise on the Preparation and Delivery of Sermons,* (Birmingham, AL: Solid Ground Christian Books, 1870), 3.

[2] The initial metaphor examples are taken from Eric Liu and Scott Noppe-Brandon, *Imagination First: Unlocking the Power of Possibility* (San Francisco, CA: Jossey-Bass, 2009), 81. The great writers understood this. Remember C.S. Lewis' essay on the Flatlanders? Lewis creates a world in which a three-dimensional person is trying to communicate to a two-dimensional being who does not possess the language or understanding to comprehend a 3D world. Lewis' conclusion on the matter: "The unknown can only be made known through metaphor" (quote taken from James Geary, *I Is an Other: The Secret Life of Metaphor and How It Shapes the Way We See the World* [New York, NY: HarperCollins Publishers, 2011], 169. Robert Frost is recorded as saying, "I have wanted in late years to go further and further in making metaphor the whole of thinking" (Geary, 35).

[3] Lakoff and Johnson, 10.

[4] In the Gutenberg era, we made a point. In the Google era, we must tell the story, show the image, and (re)sign the metaphor.

[5] This story is taken from an analysis of Benjamin Zander's TED talk in Nancy Duarte, *Resonate,* (Hoboken, NJ: John Wiley and Sons, 2010), 48-51.

[6] I got both of these SIM cards from my friend and mentor, Len Sweet. Len is a master semiotician and is an amazing resource for preachers. I encourage you to follow him on twitter @lensweet where you'll find a treasure of SIM cards.

Chapter 4

[1] A great example of the "anointing of resonance" is Brad Paisley. Regardless of your preference in music, every communicator needs to listen to Brad. He is a master story-teller whose lyrics resonate with people's lives. As you listen to a Brad Paisley song, you may find yourself nodding your head during the verses and singing along with the chorus. Actually, that's a pretty good sermon methodology. What if you structured your sermon like a country music song? Each verse is a story that resonates and the chorus is the master metaphor that people to sing along with. It's the tune that you want playing in their heads all week long.

[2] http://science.howstuffworks.com/resonance-info.htm, accessed 13 July, 2014.

[3] Ibid.

[4] http://www.youtube.com/watch?v=wvJAgrUBF4w, accessed 13 July, 2014.

[5] Ibid.

Chapter 5

[1] Conrad H. Gempf, *Jesus Asked: What He Wanted to Know* (Grand Rapids, MI: Zondervan, 2003), 25-30.

[2] John 6:5.

[3] John 6:7.

[4] John 6:5-6.

[5] In our study of all of Jesus' questions, it was discovered that forty-six times Jesus appears to ask questions for the purpose of personal introspection.

[6] Matthew 6:46.

[7] Matthew 8:26.

[8] John 6:61.

[9] Mark 8:27, 29.

[10] Luke 10:36.

[11] Luke 12:42.

[12] Matthew 21:31.

[13] Cialdini writes, "The most frequent form of classroom lecture presentation involves the description of course-relevant phenomena. A better ... approach involves the generation of mystery stories that can only be solved through an understanding of the phenomena under consideration. Although the descriptions demand attention and questions demand answers, one reason for the superiority of mystery stories is that they demand something more pedagogically valuable—explanation. By spurring students to engage in the process of providing explanation (rather than mere attention or answers), teachers offer students the best opportunity to understand psychological phenomena in a conceptual, meaningful, and enduring fashion (Cialdini, 22).

[14] The line is from Elizabeth George's *What Came Before He Shot Her* (New York, NY: HarperCollins Publishers, 2006).

[15] Lisa Cron, *Wired for Story: The Writer's Guide to Using Brain Science to Hook Readers from the Very First Sentence* (New York, NY: Ten Speed Press, 2012), 6.

[16] Annette Simmons, *Whoever Tells the Best Story Wins* (New York, NY: Amacom Publishing, 2007), 18.

[17] Larry Brooks, *Story Engineering: Mastering the 6 Core Competencies of Successful Writing* (Cincinnati, OH: Writer's Digest Books, 2011), 41-42.

[18] In the 1970s, Fred Craddock led the voice of a new movement in preaching of inductive methodology. In many ways, this was an attempt by Craddock and others to recapture the narrative and mystery elements of preaching in contrast to simply arguing propositions. See Fred B. Craddock, *As One Without Authority* (St. Louis, MO: Chalice Press, 2001); Eugene L. Lowry, *The Sermon: Dancing the Edge of Mystery* (Nashville, TN: Abingdon Press, 1997); O. Wesley Allen, ed., *The Renewed Homiletic* (Minneapolis, MN: Fortress Press, 2010).

[19] Kenneth Seeskin, *Dialogue and Discovery: A Study in Socratic Method* (Albany, NY: State University of New York Press, 1987), 1-19.

[20] "The result is, as Kierkegaard once noted, that if we do make a discovery after reading a Socratic dialogue, the credit does not go to Socrates but to us" (Ibid., 13).

[21] Seeskin himself makes (almost) this exact statement. He writes, "The purpose of elenchus is to facilitate discovery." Where then, does this author's more descriptive "enthusiastic discovery" come from? From Seeskin's own observations later in his writing. In describing Socratic dialogues, he writes, "the reader is led to believe that, like Meno's slave, [he or] she is on the verge of a great discovery... [and thus] comes away from the text with a surge of optimism." This optimism is what part of what Nietzsche refers to as "Greek cheerfulness." in his description of Socrates. Ibid., 17.

[22] Seeskin writes, "It is a cornerstone of Socratic epistemology that what people normally call teaching is impossible. That is, it is impossible to

impart true propositions to another person and expect that person to come away with knowledge." Furthermore, Seeskin goes on to state, "[Literature is] far better than expository prose for just the reason Socrates gave: expository prose puts the reader in a passive position. Literature, on the other hand, engages her, arouses her, shocks or amuses her and therefore is better suited to the goals of Socratic philosophy." Thus, for Socrates, questions were most effective and powerful when combined with story in contrast to propositional statements in combination with expository prose. Ibid., 5-7.

Chapter 6

[1] Stott, *Between Two Worlds,* 43.

[2] John 16:12-13, NLT.

[3] Matthew 16:13-15.

[4] Exodus 3:13-14.

[5] The Greek *egō eimi,* meaning "to be; to exist; to happen; to be present" is also found in Matthew 1:23, "The virgin will conceive and give birth to a son, and they will call him Immanuel (which means 'God with us')." https://www.blueletterbible.org/lang/lexicon/lexicon.cfm?Strongs=G1510&t=NIV, accessed 19 August, 2014.

[6] Another example of the power of a question would be in the context of youth ministry. For instance, as it applies to dating relationships, many students want to know, "How far is too far?" I would suggest that is the wrong question. In essence that question is, "How close can I get to sin and still go to heaven?" The right question is, "How close can I get to Jesus?" If you ask the wrong questions, it leads down the road to wrong answers. Right answers begin with right questions. By re-framing the question, you re-frame the entire discussion.

[7] Sally Lloyd-Jones, *The Jesus Storybook Bible* (Grand Rapids, MI: Zonderkidz, 2007.)

[8] Even the Apostle Paul, for all of his lawyer-like arguments and treatise, understood the proclamation of mystery: "The message I proclaim about Jesus Christ, in keeping with the revelation of the mystery hidden for long ages past, but now revealed and made known…" (Romans 16:25-26). "We declare God's wisdom, a mystery that has been hidden and that God destined for our glory before time began" (1 Corinthians 2:7). "[T]hat is, the mystery made known to me by revelation, as I have already written briefly, …then, you will be able to understand my insight into the mystery of Christ" (Ephesians 3:3-4). "Pray also for me, that whenever I speak, words may be given me so that I will fearlessly make known the mystery of the gospel" (Ephesians 6:19). "I have become its servant by the commission God gave me to present to you the word of God in its fullness—the mystery that has been kept hidden for ages and generations, but is now disclosed to the Lord's people. To them God has chosen to make known among the Gentiles the glorious riches of this mystery, which is Christ in you, the hope of glory" (Colossians 2:25-27). "And pray for us, too, that God may open a door for our message, so that we may proclaim the mystery of Christ" (Colossians 4:3).

Chapter 7

[1] D. Martyn Lloyd-Jones, *Preaching and Preachers* (Grand Rapids, MI: Zondervan, 2011), 43.

[2] Notice the SIM card. The story is of my learning to surf. The image is the wave. The metaphor is that of positioning ourselves where the wind of the Spirit pushes the water of the gospel over the landscape of culture.

[3] Biblical scholar Merril Tenney's commentary here is particularly interesting. He notes that twenty-five times in the gospel of John, Jesus

asserts himself as being sent by the Father. He goes on to say that two different words are used: "*pempō,* which means to 'send' in a broad or general sense, and *apostellō,* which has the additional connotation of 'equip,' 'commission', or 'delegate.'" (Tenney, *Expositor's,* 66.) Tenney says that in many of the occurrences the words are used interchangeably but that both appear in the last instance in John 20:21: "As the Father has sent (*aspertalkenI*) me, I am sending (*pempō*) you." He concludes, "If any real difference can be detected, Jesus is saying, "In the same way the Father commissioned me, so am I dispatching you on my errand" (Tenney, 66). What Tenney is bringing out is an expected continuation of the work of Christ through the ministry of his followers. If Jesus' purpose was to discern what the Father wanted and carry it out, then his followers should expect to continue in this pattern of ministry.

[4] John 5:17.

[5] John 5:19.

[6] John 5:30.

[7] Ronald Allen describes the premodern period as strongly rooted in tradition (which is passed on through story) and suprahuman realities (the supernatural). In contrast, "the hallmark of the modernism is respect for science and logic … [in which] many moderns disdained the past as superstitious and primitive" (Ronald J. Allen, Barbara Shires. Blaisdell, and Scott Black. Johnston, *Theology for Preaching* [Nashville, TN: Abingdon Press, 1997], 15-16).

[8] Michael Polanyi, *Personal Knowledge: Towards a Post-Critical Philosophy* (Chicago, IL: University of Chicago Press, 1958), 330.

[9] Ibid., 49-50.

[10] Polanyi, 134.

[11] Jenkins, *The Next Christendom*, 2.

[12] Jenkins states, "The global perspective should make us think carefully before asserting 'What Christians believe' or 'how the church is changing.' All too often statements about what 'modern Christians accept'... refer only to what the ever-shrinking remnant of *Western* Christians and Catholics believe. Such assertions are outrageous today, and as time goes by they will become even further removed from reality" (Ibid, 3).

[13] Ibid, 9.

[14] See summary of Jenkins' findings in Amos Yong, *The Spirit Poured Out on All Flesh: Pentecostalism and the Possibility of Global Theology* (Grand Rapids, MI: Baker Academic, 2005), 19.

[15] Ibid.

[16] Jenkins, *The Next Christendom*, 11.

Chapter 8

[1] D. Martyn Lloyd-Jones, *Preaching and Preachers,* (Grand Rapids, MI: Zondervan, 2011).

[2] Hosea 12:4, NLT.

[3] Leonard Sweet, *Giving Blood,* (Grand Rapids, MI: Zondervan, 2013).

[4] Matthew 28:6.

[5] Ephesians 1:19-20.

[6] Robert Webber, *Ancient-Future Faith: Rethinking Evangelicalism for a Postmodern World,* (Grand Rapids, MI: Baker Books, 1999).

[7] "Elisha said, ... 'But now bring me a harpist.' While the harpist was playing, the hand of the Lord came on Elisha and he said, "This is what the Lord says ..." (2 Kings 3:15-16).

[8] Matthew 4:23, NLT, emphasis added.

[9] Please hear me. I'm not saying that we cannot include emotional paralysis in our application of the message, just that we shouldn't limit it to that.

[10] Samuel Chand, *Cracking Your Church's Culture Code* (San Francisco, CA: Jossey-Bass, 2011).

[11] 1 Corinthians 1:20.

[12] 2 Kings 3:11.

[13] 2 Kings 3:12.

Chapter 9

[1] Stott, 42.

[2] Ibid., 38.

[3] Mary Douglas, *Thinking in Circles: An Essay on Ring Composition* (New Haven, CT: Yale University Press, 2007).

[4] Dr. Seuss, *Oh, the Places You'll Go!* (New York, NY: Random House, 1960).

Epilogue

[1] Russell Evans, *The Honor Key,* (Springfield, MO: My Healthy Church, 2014), 27.

[2] The account is found in Acts 5-6.

[3] John Stott, *Between Two Worlds,* (Grand Rapids, MI: Eerdmans Publishing, 1982), 50.